Raising
Cane

The Asian American Experience

THE ASIAN AMERICAN EXPERIENCE

Raising Cane

THE WORLD OF
PLANTATION HAWAII

Ronald Takaki

PROFESSOR OF ETHNIC STUDIES
THE UNIVERSITY OF CALIFORNIA AT BERKELEY

Adapted by Rebecca Stefoff

Chelsea House Publishers

New York ✳ Philadelphia

On the cover An Asian immigrant cuts sugar cane on a plantation in Hawaii.

Chelsea House Publishers

EDITORIAL DIRECTOR   Richard Rennert
EXECUTIVE MANAGING EDITOR   Karyn Gullen Browne
COPY CHIEF   Robin James
PICTURE EDITOR   Adrian G. Allen
ART DIRECTOR   Robert Mitchell
MANUFACTURING DIRECTOR   Gerald Levine
PRODUCTION COORDINATOR   Marie Claire Cebrián-Ume

The Asian American Experience

SENIOR EDITOR   Jake Goldberg
SERIES DESIGN   Marjorie Zaum

Staff for *Raising Cane*
COPY EDITOR   Catherine Iannone
EDITORIAL ASSISTANT   Kelsey Goss
PICTURE RESEARCHER   Wendy P. Wills

Adapted and reprinted from *Strangers from a Different Shore*,
© 1989 by Ronald Takaki, by arrangement with the author
and Little, Brown and Company, Inc.

First Printing
1   3   5   7   9   8   6   4   2

Library of Congress Cataloging-in-Publication Data
Takaki, Ronald T., 1939–
    Raising cane: the world of plantation Hawaii / Ronald Takaki.
        p. cm.—(Asian American experience)
    Includes bibliographical references (p.) and index.
    ISBN 0-7910-2178-5.
        0-7910-2278-1 (pbk.)
    I. Asians—Hawaii—History. 2. Alien labor—Hawaii—History. 3.
Plantation workers—Hawaii—History. 4. Sugar workers—Hawaii—
History. 5. Hawaii—Ethnic relations. 6. Asian Americans—Hawaii—
History. I. Title. II. Series: Asian American experience (New York,
N.Y.)
DU624.7.A85T35 1993   93-5307
996.9'00495—dc20   CIP
                                              AC

Contents

Hauling cane on a Hawaiian sugar plantation in the 1880s.

From a Different Shore

AS A CHILD IN HAWAII, I GREW UP IN A MULTICULTURAL corner of America. My own family had roots in Japan and China.

Grandfather Kasuke Okawa arrived in Hawaii in 1866, and my father, Toshio Takaki, came as a 13-year-old boy in 1918. My stepfather, Koon Keu Young, sailed from China to the islands when he was a teenager.

My neighbors were Japanese, Chinese, Hawaiian, Filipino, Portuguese, and Korean. Behind my house, Alice Liu and her friends played the traditional Chinese game of mahjongg late into the night, the clicking of the tiles lulling me to sleep.

Next to us the Miuras flew billowing and colorful carp kites on Japanese boy's day. I heard voices with different accents, different languages, and saw children of different colors.

Together we went barefoot to school and played games like baseball and *jan ken po*. We spoke "pidgin English," a melodious language of the streets and community. "Hey, da kind tako ono, you know," we would say, combining English, Japanese, and Hawaiian. "This octopus is delicious." Racially and culturally diverse, we all thought of ourselves as Americans.

But we did not know why families representing such an array of nationalities from different shores were living together and sharing their cultures and a common language. Our teachers and textbooks did not explain the diversity of our community or the sources of our unity.

7

After graduation from high school, I attended a college in a midwestern town where I found myself invited to "dinners for foreign students" sponsored by local churches and clubs like the Rotary. I politely tried to explain to my kind hosts that I was not a "foreign student." My fellow students and even my professors would ask me how long I had been in America and where I had learned to speak English. "In this country," I would reply. And sometimes I would add: "I was born in America, and my family has been here for three generations."

Asian Americans have been here for over 150 years. They are diverse, coming originally from countries such as China, Japan, Korea, the Philippines, India, Vietnam, Laos, and Cambodia. Many of them live in Chinatowns, the colorful streets filled with sidewalk vegetable stands and crowds of people carrying shopping bags; their communities are also called Little Tokyo, Koreatown, and Little Saigon. Asian Americans work in hot kitchens and bus tables in restaurants with elegant names like Jade Pagoda and Bombay Spice. In garment factories, Chinese and Korean women hunch over whirling sewing machines, their babies sleeping nearby on blankets. In the Silicon Valley of California, rows and rows of Vietnamese and Laotian women serve as the eyes and hands of production assembly lines for computer chip industries. Tough Chinese gang members strut on Grant Avenue in San Francisco and Canal Street in New York's Chinatown. In La Crosse, Wisconsin, Hmong refugees from Laos, now dependent on welfare, sit and stare at the snowdrifts outside their windows. Asian American engineers do complex research in the laboratories of the high-technology industries along

Route 128 in Massachusetts. Asian Americans seem to be everywhere on university campuses.

Today, Asian Americans belong to the fastest growing ethnic group in the United States. Kept out of the United States by immigration restriction laws in the 19th and early 20th centuries, Asians have recently been coming again to America. The 1965 immigration act reopened the gates to immigrants from Asia, allowing 20,000 immigrants from each country to enter every year. In the early 1990s, half of all immigrants entering annually are Asian.

The growth of the Asian American population has been dramatic: In 1960, there were only 877,934 Asians in the United States, representing a mere one half of 1% of the American people. Thirty years later, they numbered about seven million or 3% of the population. They included 1,645,000 Chinese, 1,400,000 Filipinos, 845,000 Japanese, 815,000 Asian Indians, 800,000 Koreans, 614,000 Vietnamese, 150,000 Laotians, 147,000 Cambodians, and 90,000 Hmong. By the year 2000, Asian Americans will probably represent 4% of the total United States population. In California, Asian Americans already make up 10% of the state's inhabitants, compared with 7.5% for African Americans.

Yet very little is known about Asian Americans and their history. Many existing history books give Asian Americans only passing notice—or overlook them entirely. "When one hears Americans tell of the immigrants who built this nation," Congressman Norman Mineta of California observed, "one is often led to believe that all our forebearers came from Europe. When one hears stories about the pioneers going West to shape the land, the Asian immigrant is rarely mentioned."

Indeed, many history books have equated "American" with "white" or "European" in origin. In his prize-winning study, *The Uprooted*, Harvard historian Oscar Handlin presented—to use the book's subtitle—"the Epic Story of the Great Migrations that Made the American People." But Handlin's "epic story" completely left out the "uprooted" from lands across the Pacific Ocean and the "great migrations" from Asia that also helped to make "the American people." As Americans, we have origins in Europe, the Americas, Africa, and also Asia.

We need to include Asians in the history of America. How and why, we ask in this series, were the experiences of these various groups—Chinese, Japanese, Korean, Filipino, Asian Indian, and Southeast Asian—similar to and different from each other? Comparing the experiences of different nationalities can help us see what events were particular to a group and also highlight the experiences they all shared.

Why did Asian immigrants leave everything they knew and loved to come to a strange world so far away? They were "pushed" by hardships in the homelands and "pulled" by demands for their labor in Canada, Brazil, and especially the United States. But what were their own fierce dreams—from the first enterprising Chinese miners of the 1850s in search of "Gold Mountain" to the recent refugees fleeing frantically on helicopters and leaking boats from the ravages of war in Vietnam?

Besides their points of origin, we need to examine the experiences of Asian Americans in different geographical regions, especially Hawaii compared with the mainland. The time of arrival also shaped their lives and communities. About one million people entered the United States between the California gold rush of 1849 and the 1924 immigration act that cut off the flow of peoples from Asian countries. After a break of some 40 years, a second group numbering about four million came between 1965 and 1990. How do we compare the two waves of Asian immigration?

To answer our questions in these volumes, we must study Asian Americans as men and women with minds, wills, and voices. By "voices" we mean their own words and stories as told in their oral histories, conversations, speeches, and songs as well as their own writings—diaries, letters, newspapers, novels, and poems. We need to know the ordinary people.

So much of history has been the story of kings and elites, as if the "little people" were invisible and voiceless. An Asian American told an interviewer: "I am a second generation Korean American without any achievements in life and I have no education. What is it you want to hear from me? My life is not worth telling to anyone." Similarly, a Chinese immigrant said: "You know, it seems to me there's no use in me telling you all this! I was just a simple worker, a farm worker around here. My story is not going to interest anybody." But others realize they are worthy of attention. "What is it you want to know?" an old Filipino immigrant asked a researcher. "Talk about history. What's that . . . ah, the story of my life . . . and how people lived with each other in my time."

Their stories can enable us to understand Asians as actors in the making of history and as people entitled to dignity. "I hope this survey do a lot of good for Chinese people," a Chinese man told an interviewer from Stanford

University in the 1920s. "Make American people realize that Chinese people are humans. I think very few American people really know anything about Chinese." Elderly Asians want the younger generations to know about their experiences. "Our stories should be listened to by many young people," said a 91-year-old retired Japanese plantation laborer. "It's for their sake. We really had a hard time, you know."

The stories of Asian immigrations belong to our country's history. They need to be recorded in our history books, for they reflect the making of America as a nation of immigrants, as a place where men and women came to find a new beginning. At first, many Asian immigrants—probably most of them—saw themselves as sojourners, or temporary migrants. Like many European immigrants such as the Italians and Greeks, they came to America thinking they would be here only a short time. They had left their wives and children behind in their homelands. Their plan was to work here for a few years and then return home with money. But, after their arrival, many found themselves staying. They became settlers instead of remaining sojourners. Bringing their families to their adopted country, they began putting down new roots in America.

But, coming here from Asia, many of America's immigrants found they were not allowed to feel at home in the United States. Even their grandchildren and great-grandchildren still find they are not viewed and accepted as Americans. "We feel that we're a guest in someone else's house," said third generation Ron Wakabayashi, National Director of the Japanese American Citizens League, "that we can never really relax and put our feet on the table."

Behind Wakabayashi's complaint is the question: Why have Asian Americans been considered outsiders? America's immigrants from Pacific shores found they were forced to remain strangers in the new land. Their experiences here were profoundly different from the experiences of European immigrants. Asian immigrants had qualities they could not change or hide—the shape of their eyes, the color of their hair, the complexion of their skins. They were subjected not only to cultural and ethnic prejudice but also to racism. Unlike the Irish and other groups from Europe, Asian immigrants were not treated as individuals but as members of a group with distinctive physical characteristics. Regardless of their personal merits, they sadly discovered, they could not gain acceptance in the larger society.

Unlike European immigrants, Asians were victimized by laws and policies that discriminated on the basis of race. The Chinese Exclusion Act of 1882 barred the Chinese from coming to America because they were Chinese. The National Origins Act of 1924 totally prohibited Japanese immigration.

The laws determined not only who could come to America but also who could become citizens. Decades before Asian immigration began, the United States had already defined the complexion of its citizens: the Naturalization Law of 1790 had specified that naturalized citizenship was to be reserved for "whites." This law remained in effect until 1952. Unlike white ethnic immigrants from countries like Ireland, Asian immigrants were denied citizenship and also the right to vote.

But America also had an opposing tradition and vision, springing from the reality of racial and cultural "diversity." Ours has been, as Walt Whitman celebrated so lyrically, "a teeming Nation of nations" composed of a "vast, surging, hopeful army of workers," a new society where all should be welcomed, "Chinese, Irish, German,—all, all, without exceptions." In the early 20th century, a Japanese immigrant described in poetry a lesson that had been learned by farm laborers of different nationalities—Japanese, Filipino, Mexican, and Asian Indian:

> *People harvesting*
> *Work together unaware*
> *Of racial problems.*

A Filipino immigrant laborer in California expressed a similar hope and understanding. America was, Macario Bulosan told his brother Carlos, "not a land of one race or one class of men" but "a new world" of respect and unconditional opportunities for all who toiled and suffered from oppression, from "the first Indian that offered peace in Manhattan to the last Filipino pea pickers." Asian immigrants came here, as one of them expressed it, searching for "a door into America" and seeking "to build a new life with untried materials." He asked: "Would it be possible for an immigrant like me to become a part of the American dream?"

This series invites students to learn how Asian Americans belong to the larger story of the rich multicultural mosaic called the United States of America.

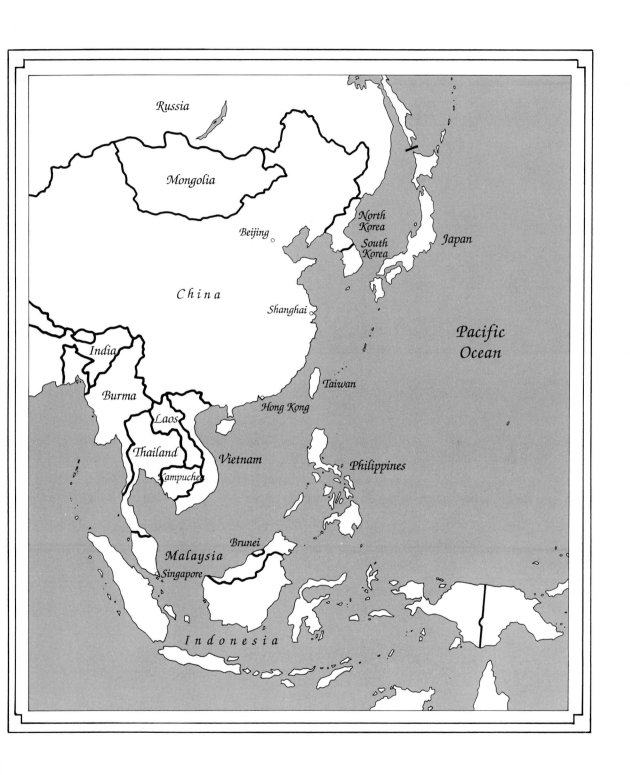

The arrival of Captain James Cook's two ships in 1778 signaled the opening of Hawaii to the outside world. Traders, missionaries, and colonizers soon followed Cook to the islands.

Chapter One

Sandalwood
and
Sugar Cane

WHEN NOONTIME CAME, STUDENTS AT THE SCHOOL ON the Waialua Plantation in Hawaii shared a daily ritual. Each boy and girl had brought a lunch to school. When it was time to eat, they mingled in the schoolyard and traded lunches. Portuguese children swapped jelly or cheese sandwiches for their Japanese schoolmates' lunches of *musubi*, rice balls with pickled red plums inside them. Savoring the tasty treats, each child felt that he or she had made a good trade.

Meanwhile, at work on the plantation, their parents were doing the same thing. In the fields of sugar cane, they shared their meals. "We get in a group," one man explained. "We pick from this guy's lunch, and that guy'll pick from my lunch and so forth." Filipino laborers brought their traditional meal of salted fish and rice. Koreans had kimchi, pickled cabbage laced with garlic and hot red pepper. Japanese workers had their musubi; Portuguese workers had sandwiches. Chinese offerings might include buns stuffed with pork. Together the workers shared a meal that combined the foods of many countries and many peoples. As they sat in the schoolyards and fields, swapping lunches and jokes under the hot sun, the people of plantation Hawaii were creating a richly multicultural society.

Until the late 18th century, the Hawaiian Islands had been unknown to Asians, Europeans, and Americans. But in 1778 Captain James Cook, exploring the Pacific Ocean for Britain, bumped into the island chain, which he called the Sandwich Islands after a British nobleman. As soon as word of Cook's "discovery" spread, European and American sea captains began landing in Hawaii.

17

They found a land of extraordinary beauty. The Hawaiian Islands are a chain of volcanic peaks that rise steeply from the Pacific Ocean floor and are ringed by coral reefs. The largest of the seven inhabited islands is Hawaii, called the Big Island. Maui, Molokai, Oahu, and Kauai are smaller than Hawaii; and Lanai and Niihau are smaller still. These fertile islands were settled by the Polynesians, Pacific seafarers who crossed the ocean in huge, skillfully made canoes. Between the 6th and the 13th centuries, Polynesians from Tahiti and the Marquesas—islands far to the south—reached Hawaii in several waves of migration. By the time Cook arrived, these settlers had formed the Hawaiian culture, with its own language and religion. When whites—*haoles,* or outsiders, as the Hawaiians called them—first came to Hawaii, the islands were covered with luxuriant tropical forest. The scented trees that grew on the sheer, rugged mountainsides gave Hawaii its Chinese nickname: *Tan Heung Shan,* the Fragrant Sandalwood Hills. Western ships carried the sweet-smelling sandalwood timber to China, where it was greatly prized, especially for the making of coffins and fans. The ship captains hired Chinese men to serve in their crews, and thus Chinese sailors made their way to Hawaii. The first Chinese arrived in the islands as early as 1789.

At that time, the islands were divided into four kingdoms. King Kamehameha I came to the throne of one of these kingdoms in 1782. By 1795 he had unified them into a single realm, which he ruled until his death in 1819. The sandalwood trade flourished during Kamehameha's reign. It was so profitable that all the sandalwood was harvested; there is none in Hawaii today.

After Kamehameha's death, Western influence became much stronger in the islands. The first Christian missionaries reached Hawaii in 1820. They were followed by traders, naval officers, travelers, and adventurers from the United States, Great Britain, and France.

The arrival of outsiders changed Hawaii forever, but one American visitor helped shape Hawaii's future in a particular way. He was William Hooper, a young man from Boston. Hooper came in 1835 to clear land, plant sugar cane, and start Hawaii's first sugar plantation on the island of Kauai. Wild sugar cane was already being harvested there, but Hooper was the first to cultivate the cane on an orderly plantation carved out of the forest. Hooper's experiment was a success. Other planters followed his example, and soon sugar cane was being grown all over the islands. Later, pineapple plantations also dotted the hillsides and valleys as more forest was cleared and the land was put under cultivation.

By introducing plantation farming into Hawaii, Hooper changed the landscape of the islands. He also changed their ethnic mix. He hired Chinese workers for his sugar mill, and once again other planters followed his example. He had set the stage for a large-scale migration of Asian men and women into Hawaii.

"Get labor first," the early sugar planters in Hawaii said. With enough workers they would make profits, which could be used to buy more land, plant more sugar, and hire more workers. During the second half of the 19th century, these American businessmen and sons of American missionaries made Hawaii into an economic colony of the United States.

King Kamehameha I, as drawn by a member of a Russian exploring expedition in 1816. The king united Hawaii into a single kingdom, which lasted for almost a century before the United States took control of the islands.

Throughout the 19th century, the United States increased its influence and investment in Hawaii until, in 1898, the U.S. took control of the islands. Hawaii officially became an American territory two years later (although it did not become a state until 1959). By the beginning of the 20th century, Hawaii's economy was closely bound to that of the United States. Importing sugar to the mainland was Hawaii's biggest business. Years of back-breaking effort had turned Hawaii into a productive plantation colony. Much of that work was done by "strangers from a different shore"—from China and also from Japan, Korea, and the Philippines.

To help turn the islands into a plantation colony, the planters arranged the 1875 Reciprocity Treaty between the governments of Hawaii and the United States. This treaty permitted Hawaii to sell sugar to the United States without paying duties, or import taxes. Cane growing thus became very profitable. More and more money was invested in plantations, and the production of sugar skyrocketed from 9,400 tons in 1870 to nearly 300,000 tons in 1900. Between 1875 and 1910, the amount of land cultivated for cane plantations multiplied nearly 18 times, from 12,000 acres to 214,000 acres.

Sugar was "King" in Hawaii, as an island newspaper exulted in 1877. But to be king, the sugar industry needed a constant supply of labor for the plantations. The planters could not rely on the labor of Kanakas, as Hawaiian men were called. There were simply not enough native workers—the Hawaiian population had been dropping sharply, largely because Hawaiians had never developed resistance to the diseases of the whites. Many Hawaiians died of measles and smallpox. In addition, Hawaiian workers were not easily

*Spearfishing on Oahu in the 1890s. The native Hawaiians had no need
of a plantation wage; they lived on the harvest of the sea and their gardens.
Planters had to bring workers from elsewhere, and they turned to Asia
to meet the need for labor.*

disciplined. They could not be threatened with the loss of their jobs, because they could live comfortably by farming and fishing.

So the planters followed William Hooper's lead and turned to Chinese labor. In 1850 they founded the Royal Hawaiian Agricultural Society to bring workers from China. The Chinese were not the only group brought to Hawaii to work in the cane fields. In the years to come, the planters would look all over the world, including Europe, for workers. But they looked mainly to Asia.

Why did Asian workers come to Hawaii? Some came to escape poverty, famine, or political turmoil in their homelands. Many were enticed by the seemingly high plantation wages—more money than they could earn at home. And some of the labor migrants were stirred by a longing for change, a sense of adventure. Most of them expected to stay in Hawaii for only a few years. Then they would proudly return home with the money they had earned in the islands.

In the 19th century, most Asian migrants came to Hawaii as contract laborers. They signed labor contracts with brokers who represented the sugar planters. In signing the contracts, laborers agreed to work for a set period, usually three years or five years. In return, they received passage to Hawaii as well as wages, shelter, food, and medical care during the contract period.

The contract labor system ended in 1900, when Hawaii officially became a U.S. territory, because it was banned under American law. But Asian migrants continued to come to Hawaii as free laborers. They used their savings or money from their families to buy their tickets, or they paid their fares under the credit-ticket system, borrowing the passage money and then paying off the loan, plus interest, from their earnings in the new land.

When they arrived in Hawaii, workers were assigned to plantations by supply companies in Honolulu, the capital of the islands, located on Oahu. Planters sent these suppliers lists of what they needed. The planters regarded laborers as necessary equipment, just like hoes and horses. One planter's order included these items:

Japanese laborers
canvas
a Chinaman

Chinese immigrants arrive in Honolulu to work on the sugar plantations. Hawaii's prosperity was built on the labor of Asian workers.

macaroni

Another planter's order listed his needs alphabetically:

Fertilizer

Filipinos

When they ordered laborers, the planters were careful to build a work force from many different ethnic backgrounds. They did this not because they prized ethnic diversity for its own sake, but because it was easier for them to control a work force made up of different nationalities.

In the 1850s, the planters used the hard-working Chinese to set an "example" for the Hawaiian workers. Plantation managers hoped the Hawaiians would be "naturally jealous" of the foreigners and "ambitious" to outdo them. The managers encouraged the Chinese to call the native workers *"wahine! wahine!"*—Hawaiian for "women! women!"

At first, the planters got good results by pitting the Chinese against the Hawaiian workers. The Chinese worked hard, as the planters had expected. But the planters became dependent upon the Chinese laborers, who soon outnumbered the Hawaiians. The Chinese eventually wanted higher wages. The planters had to find a new source of workers they could use to control the Chinese.

They turned to Portuguese and then to Japanese workers. The Japanese newcomers, in particular, were paid lower wages than the Chinese, which meant that the Chinese were forced to continue as cheap laborers or lose their jobs to the Japanese. By the 1890s, the islands' work force consisted mostly of Japanese. Then, fearful of becoming too dependent upon the Japanese, the planters began mixing Chinese and Japanese laborers. They encouraged the two groups to view each other as rivals. By setting them against one another, the planters made each group work harder and obey orders more readily.

The planters used ethnic diversity to keep workers from uniting to demand higher pay or better working conditions. If workers were mostly from the same country, they could easily act together to form labor unions or organize strikes. But workers of different nationalities found it harder to communicate, and in some cases there were ethnic rivalries between them. Members of different groups were less likely to act together. One plantation manager told his fellow planters to hire as many different nationalities as possible to "offset" the power of any one group. Bluntly outlining the planters' divide-and-rule plan, another manager advised, "Keep a variety of laborers . . . for there are few, if any, cases of Japs, Chinese, and Portuguese entering into a strike as a unit."

After Hawaii became a United States territory, laws that had been passed to keep Chinese from immigrating to the U.S. mainland also applied to the islands. Planters could no longer import Chinese laborers. Worried that the "Japs" were "getting too numerous," the planters looked for new sources of labor. They turned to Korea, planning to pit Korean workers against Japanese workers.

Korean workers were introduced to the plantations in 1903. Because Japan and Korea were then in conflict, the Japanese and Korean people were hostile toward one another. The planters could be pretty sure that the Korean laborers were "not likely to combine with the Japanese at any attempt at strikes." One planter, angry at his Japanese workers for demanding higher wages, asked a labor company to send him a shipment of Korean workers, saying, "In our opinion, it

Japanese workers line up in Honolulu, waiting to be assigned to their plantations. Plantation managers ordered workers in the same way that they ordered supplies such as rope, canvas, and machinery.

would be advisable, as soon as circumstances permit, to get a large number of Koreans in the country . . . and drive the Japs out."

But just as the supply of Chinese labor had been cut off by U.S. immigration laws, the Korean labor supply ended when the government of Korea banned emigration to Hawaii in 1905. Once again, the planters had to find a new source of workers. This time they turned to the Philippine Islands, which, like Hawaii, had been taken over by the United States in 1898.

The first Filipino laborers arrived in Hawaii in 1906. A labor recruiter paraded them on the dock in Honolulu, promising that the Filipino would be a "first-class laborer," "possibly not as good as the Chinaman or the Jap, but steady, faithful and willing to do his best for any boss for whom he has a liking."

Soon the planters were importing massive numbers of Filipino workers. Like the Chinese and Koreans, the Filipinos were used by the planters to control and discipline the Japanese workers. One planter, complaining that his Japanese workers were demanding higher wages, wrote to a labor company, "If possible for you to arrange it I should very much like to get say 25 new Filipinos to put into our day gang. . . . In this way perhaps we can stir the Japs a bit."

In all, more than 300,000 immigrants from Asia came to Hawaii between 1850 and 1920. Their presence made the islands much more ethnically diverse than the American mainland. At the beginning of this great wave of Asian immigration, 97% of the islands' inhabitants were Hawaiian or part-Hawaiian, 2% were white, and only one-half of 1% were Chinese. But 70 years later, 62% of the island population was Asian, and only 16% was Hawaiian or part-Hawaiian. Of the total population in 1920, 43% were Japanese, 19% were white (more than half of these were Portuguese plantation workers), 9% were Chinese, 8% were Filipino, 2% were Korean, and 2% were Puerto Ricans. The Asian presence was far smaller on the American mainland. In 1920, Asians made up less than 4% of California's population and less than one-fifth of 1% of the total U.S. population.

In their eagerness to make fortunes from the fertile volcanic soil, the sugar planters of Hawaii imported so many workers from Asia that Asians became the majority of Hawaii's population. In their determination to control these workers, the planters used ethnic diversity as a tool. The planters hoped for ethnic rivalry, but friendship and cooperation also took root in the labor camps as people shared their meals, their troubles, and their lives. The world of plantation Hawaii became a uniquely multicultural society.

A Japanese woman stacking stalks of sugar cane. Japanese women frequently worked in the cane fields.

Chapter Two

Hana-hana: Working

Hawaii, Hawaii
Like a dream
So I came
But my tears
Are flowing now
In the canefields.

AS THIS PLANTATION WORK SONG SAYS, HAWAII DID
not always fulfill the dreams and hopes of the Asian immigrants. Many of them were not prepared for plantation life.
They came from societies where they worked not for bosses
but for their own families. In their homelands, life was shaped
by traditions, by well-known rules and obligations. People
worked with family members or fellow villagers, and they
controlled their time and their activities. "In Japan," a plantation laborer said, "we could say, 'It's okay to take the day
off today,' since it was our own work. We were free to do
what we wanted. We didn't have that freedom on the plantation. We had to work ten hours every day." *Hana-hana*, as
plantation work was called in Hawaiian, was very different
from the work most of the immigrants had known.

On the plantation, laborers were aroused by the loud
screams of a plantation siren at five in the morning. One work
song captured this moment:

> *"Awake! stir your bones! Rouse up!*
> *Shrieks the Five o'Clock Whistle.*
> *"Don't dream you can nestle*
> *For one more sweet nap.*
> *Or your ear-drums I'll rap*

With my steam-hammer tap
Till they burst.
Br-r-row-aw-i-e-ur-ur-rup!
Wake up! wake up! wake up! w-a-k-e-u-u-u-up!
Filipino and Japanee;
Porto Rican and Portugee;
Korean, Kanaka and Chinese;
Everybody whoever you be
On the whole plantation—
Wake up! wake up! wake up! w-a-k-e-u-u-u-up!
Br-r-row-aw-i-e-ur-ur-rup!

After the five A.M. plantation whistle had blown, the *lunas,* or foremen, and company policemen strode through the camps. "Get up, get up," they shouted as they knocked on the doors of the cottages and the barracks. "Hana-hana, hana-hana, work, work." A Korean woman remembered the morning her mother failed to hear the work whistle and overslept: "We were all asleep—my brother and his wife, my older sister, and myself. Suddenly the door swung open, and a big burly luna burst in, screaming and cursing, 'Get up, get to work.' The luna ran around the room, ripping off the covers, not caring whether my family was dressed or not."

A Filipino laborer had similar memories. "You must wake up," he said, or a policeman would kick open the door of your room and chase you out of bed. One day, one of his companions decided to stay in bed. The worker recalled: "Oh, the policeman come, and my friend was so scared that he ran to work in his underpants."

A visitor to Hawaii described how "the workers on a plantation in all their tongues and kindreds, 'rolled out' sometime in the early morn, before the break of day." One by one and two by two, laborers appeared from "the shadows, like a brigade of ghosts." From an outlying camp, they came by train, "car after car of silent figures," their cigarettes glowing in the darkness. They lined up in front of the mill, shouldering their hoes. As the sun rose, "quietly the word was passed from somewhere in the dimness. Suddenly and silently the gang started for its work, dividing themselves with one accord to the four quarters of the compass, each heading toward his daily task."

In gangs of 20 to 30 workers, the laborers marched or were carried by wagons and trains to the fields. Each gang was watched by a luna. Almost all the lunas were haoles, or whites. Some work gangs were made up of one nationality, while others were mixed. One luna said he had workers of all races in his gang, including Hawaiians, Filipinos, Puerto Ricans, Chinese, Japanese, Portuguese, and Koreans.

There were gangs of women workers, too, for women were part of the plantation work force. In 1894, about 7% of all workers were women. By 1920, 14% were women. More than four-fifths of the women workers were Japanese. Women were concentrated in field operations, such as hoeing, stripping leaves, and harvesting. My grandmother Katsu Okawa was a cane cutter, and my aunt Yukino Takaki was a cane loader. Though women were given many of the same work assignments as men, they were paid less than the men. Japanese women field hands, for example, received an average wage of only 55 cents a day in 1915, compared with 78 cents for Japanese men.

Women worked in the camps as well as in the fields. They washed laundry, cooked, and sewed clothes. "I made

Cutting cane was backbreaking work. Despite the stifling heat, workers wore heavy clothing to protect themselves from the saw-edged cane leaves.

custom shirts with hand-bound button holes for 25 cents," recalled a Korean woman. "My mother and sister-in-law took in laundry. They scrubbed, ironed and mended shirts for a nickel a piece. It was pitiful! Their knuckles became swollen and raw from using the harsh yellow soap." My grandmother Katsu Okawa operated a boarding house where she fed her husband and eight children as well as fifteen men every day.

Field work was strictly ordered, like being in the army. "We worked like machines," a laborer complained. "For 200 of us workers, there were seven or eight lunas and above them was a field boss on a horse. We were watched constantly." A Japanese woman, interviewed years later at the age of 91, said, "We had to work in the canefields, cutting cane, being afraid, not knowing the language. When any *haole* or Portuguese luna came, we got frightened and thought we had to work harder or get fired."

Another Japanese worker recalled, "The *luna* carried a whip and rode a horse. If we talked too much the man swung the whip. He did not actually whip us but just swung his whip so that we would work harder." A Korean woman fumed, "I'll never forget the foreman. He said we worked like 'lazy.' He wanted us to work faster. He would gallop around on horseback and crack and snap his whip."

One of the most tedious and backbreaking tasks was hoeing weeds. Laborers had to "hoe hoe hoe . . . for four hours in a straight line and no talking," said a worker. "Hoe every weed along the way to your three rows. Hoe—chop chop chop, one chop for one small weed, two for all big ones." Workers had to keep their bodies bent over. Something as simple as standing up and stretching the knots out of their twisted bodies and aching backs was a forbidden pleasure.

The laborers cursed the lunas and the driving pace of the work. One worker said, "It burns us up to have an ignorant *luna* stand around and holler and swear at us all the time for not working fast enough. Every so often, just to show how good he is, he'll come up and grab a hoe and work like hell for about two minutes and then say sarcastically, 'Why you no work like that?' He knows and we know he couldn't work for ten minutes at that pace."

Laborers also did "hole hole" work, stripping the dead leaves from the cane stalks. Each leaf was edged with sharp needles, like a little saw. To protect themselves from these needles, the workers wore heavy clothing. Still, as they left the fields each day, they found their hands badly cut by the cane blades. In a work song, Japanese laborers lamented:

Raising Cane

Hawaii, Hawaii
But when I came
What I saw
Was hell
The boss was Satan
The lunas
His helpers.

As they worked, laborers wore *bangos* on chains around their necks. These were small brass disks with their identification numbers stamped on them. In the old country, the workers had names that connected them to their families and communities. In Hawaii, they were given numbers. The workers resented this new, impersonal identity. Laborers were

By the 1890s, the large plantations were using engines rather than ox carts to move workers and cane to and from the fields.

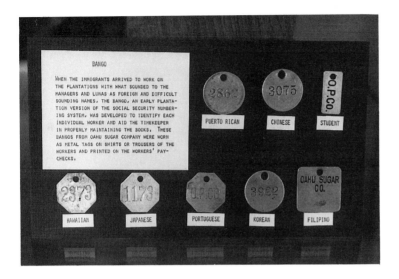

BANGO

WHEN THE IMMIGRANTS ARRIVED TO WORK ON
THE PLANTATIONS WITH WHAT SOUNDED TO THE
MANAGERS AND LUNAS AS FOREIGN AND DIFFICULT
SOUNDING NAMES, THE BANGO, AN EARLY PLANTA-
TION VERSION OF THE SOCIAL SECURITY NUMBER-
ING SYSTEM, WAS DEVELOPED TO IDENTIFY EACH
INDIVIDUAL WORKER AND AID THE TIMEKEEPER
IN PROPERLY MAINTAINING THE BOOKS. THESE
BANGOS FROM OAHU SUGAR COMPANY WERE WORN
AS METAL TAGS ON SHIRTS OR TROUSERS OF THE
WORKERS AND PRINTED ON THE WORKERS' PAY-
CHECKS.

PUERTO RICAN   CHINESE   STUDENT

HAWAIIAN   JAPANESE   PORTUGUESE   KOREAN   FILIPINO

"treated no better than cows or horses," one of them recalled. "Every worker was called by number, never by name." The lunas "never called a man by his name," another worker grumbled. "Always by the bango, 7209 or 6508 in that manner. And that was the thing I objected to. I wanted my name, not the number."

When the cane was ripe, lunas on horseback led the workers out into the fields to harvest the crop. A visitor described the harvest this way: "Just beyond these Chinese huts were canefields, an intense yellow-green, the long, slender leaves tossing in the breeze like a maize-field before the harvest. There were great bands of Japanese at work in the field." They worked with "incredible rapidity, the line of men crossing a field, levelling the cane."

Cutting the ripe cane was dirty and exhausting work. As the workers mechanically swung the long knives called machetes, they felt the pain of the blisters on their hands and

Because white managers thought Asian names were hard to remember and pronounce, workers were given identity numbers, which they wore on tags called bangos. Bosses addressed workers by number, not by name, and the workers hated this indignity.

35

A rare break in the Maui cane fields. During such moments, laborers from different lands shared meals, jokes, and experiences, forming bonds across ethnic lines.

the scratches on their arms. Their heavy arms and bent backs begged for a break, a moment of rest.

> Becoming weary
> I sit for a while to rest
> In the cane field,
> And whistle
> To call the breezes.

But the breezes did not always come. Twelve feet tall, the cane stalks enclosed and dwarfed the Asian workers. Clearing the cane forests, cutting the stalks close to the ground, the workers felt the heat of the sun and the humidity of the air. They also found themselves surrounded by iron-red clouds of dust. They covered their faces with handkerchiefs; still they breathed the dust. "The sugar cane fields were endless and the stalks were twice the height of myself," a Korean woman sighed. "Now that I look back, I thank goodness for the height, for if I had seen how far the fields stretched, I probably would have fainted from knowing how much work was ahead. My waistline got slimmer and my back ached from bending over all the time to cut the sugar cane."

> *My husband cuts the cane stalks*
> *And I trim their leaves*
> *With sweat and tears we both work*
> *For our means.*

Collecting the cane stalks, the workers tied them into bundles and loaded them onto railway cars. A train then pulled the cane to the mill where engines, presses, furnaces, boilers, and other machines crushed the cane and boiled its juices into molasses and sugar. Inside the mill, laborers like my uncle Nobuyoshi Takaki felt like they were in the "hold of a steamer." They were deafened by the constant loud clanking and whirring of the machinery, and they dripped with sweat from the hellish heat of the steam.

At 4:30 in the afternoon, the workers again heard the ear-splitting blast of the plantation whistle. This time it was the signal to stop working. "*Pau hana,*" they sighed, "finished working." They were exhausted, too tired to hoe another row of cane or carry another bundle of stalks, but they suddenly felt a final burst of energy and eagerly scrambled back to the camps.

> *In the rush at pau hana*
> *I get caught in cane leaves,*
> *When I stumble and fall,*
> *They prickle, they jab.*

Field bosses and office workers on a Kauai plantation in 1911.
Nearly all supervisors were whites, while most laborers were Asian.
Racial discrimination kept Asian workers from advancing to better
jobs on the plantations.

Chapter Three

Planters and Workers

THE PLANTERS OF HAWAII CLAIMED THAT THEY treated their workers well, seeking in "every possible way to advance their comfort and make them contented and happy." But the planters had reasons of their own for treating the workers well and keeping them happy. They had learned that it was "good business" to have their workers "properly fed." A "contented lot of laborers" would produce a "good day's work."

The planters also knew that if they did not take care of the workers, the workers might organize into unions to seek better conditions and higher wages. "We should avail to get our house in order before a storm breaks," planters told themselves. Contented workers would have less reason to join together in labor movements. The planters agreed that "humanity in industry pays."

The population of the plantation was divided by race. The plantation managers and foremen were white. The work force was mostly nonwhite—70% to 85% Asian. The owners and managers believed themselves to be naturally superior to the Asians because they were white. They saw their role as "parental." To them, the Koreans were "childlike" and the Filipinos were "more or less like children." One labor supplier warned plantation managers that the Filipino was "very incapable of caring for himself." Left entirely to his own resources, the Filipino was likely to spend his money on "fancy groceries" and would become undernourished. As representatives of "Caucasian civilization" and the "stronger race," the whites claimed that it was their duty to supervise and "look after" their Asian and Hawaiian laborers.

But in giving themselves the responsibility of "caring for" the workers, the planters also claimed the right to control the workers—by force, if necessary. Planters believed in "the strong hand." They declared, "There is one word which holds the lower classes . . . in check, and that is Authority." One plantation bulletin compared the plantation to an army, with the manager as the general, the overseers as lieutenants and majors, and the workers as common soldiers.

Like army generals, the plantation managers expected their "troops" to follow an intricate set of rules and regulations. They required their workers to be "industrious and docile and obedient," "regular and clean in their personal habits," and always punctual for work and rest. The workers were not allowed to leave the plantations. To punish workers for breaking these rules, planters developed an elaborate system of fines. Almost every kind of misconduct had its price. On one plantation, workers were fined according to the following schedule:

> breaking wagon through negligence—$5
> refusal to do work as ordered—25 cents
> trespass—50 cents
> cutting harness—$2
> insubordination—$1
> neglect of duty—50 cents
> drunkenness—50 cents
> drunken brawling—$5
> gambling in Japanese or Chinese camps—$5

If fines did not work, the planters used harsher penalties. Asked how he would punish a contract laborer for idleness, a planter replied, "We dock him; we give him one one-half or three quarters of a day of wages; and if he keeps it up we resort to the law and have him arrested for refusing to work." Sometimes planters used physical punishment to intimidate the workers. Chinese workers on one plantation were given five to fifteen minutes for lunch, and they were kicked if they did not return promptly to work. A laborer complained about the strictness of a German luna: "If anyone violated his orders, he was punished, usually with a slap on the face."

The Hawaiian government had outlawed whipping, but the law was not always followed in the fields. One plantation manager said that disobedient "Japs" should be whipped, claiming that the Japanese had "no feelings except through the hide." In 1879, planter George Dole asked his agent about a "black snake whip" he had ordered for one of his overseers, saying, "If you have received it, please forward it." A Korean migrant bitterly recalled how he and his fellow Korean workers were not allowed to talk, smoke, or even stretch their backs as they labored in the fields: "A foreman kept his eyes on his workers at all times. When he found anyone violating working regulations, he whipped the violator without mercy." Another worker said that "life on a planta-tion is much like life in a prison."

The best jobs, the supervisory positions or those requiring skills, were reserved for whites. In 1882, for exam-ple, 88% of all lunas and clerks were white. Most laborers were nonwhite: 29% were Hawaiian and 48% were Chinese. None of the lunas were Chinese.

In 1904, the Hawaiian Sugar Planters' Association limited skilled positions to "American citizens, or those eli-gible for citizenship." Asians could not hold skilled jobs because they could not become citizens, according to a 1790

After electricity was introduced, mills were modernized with powerful new equipment. Hawaii's output of sugar soared in the early 20th century.

federal law that limited American citizenship to white people. By 1914, the planters' restriction was still in force. There were only 1 Japanese, 1 Hawaiian, and 2 part-Hawaiian mill engineers; the remaining 41 mill engineers were of European ancestry. The racial division was especially visible in the supervisors' jobs. Of the 377 overseers, 313 were white. Only 2 were Chinese and 17 Japanese.

A Japanese worker bluntly explained why he and other Japanese would never get ahead on the plantation. Told by an interviewer that he would be promoted, the worker retorted: "Don't kid me. You know yourself I haven't got a chance. You can't go very high up and get big money unless your skin is white. You can work here all your life and yet a haole who doesn't know a thing about the work can be ahead of you in no time."

After 1900, when the contract labor system was abolished, the Hawaiian Sugar Planters' Association schemed to keep workers' wages low. The association urged plantation managers to agree on the wages they would pay their workers. If wages were the same everywhere, workers would not be able to leave one plantation to look for better pay elsewhere. To carry out this plan, the association founded a central labor bureau to coordinate the employment of all Asian laborers and to set wage rates. Laborers were warned not to leave their assigned plantations to bargain for higher wages, for they would not be hired by another plantation unless they could show a certificate of discharge.

The association also introduced a "bonus system." Officials of the association said that the bonuses were rewards for "loyal labor" and "faithful service." In addition, the bonuses boosted productivity, for laborers would work harder if they expected cash rewards. But the bonus system also kept workers from leaving their plantations. The bonus was paid only once a year, and workers forfeited it if they left the plantation before bonus time. One manager stated frankly in a letter that the bonus was "a string" holding the workers to their jobs.

The planters tied other strings to their workers as well. They paid different wages to different nationalities for the same work. For example, Japanese cane cutters were paid 99 cents a day, while Filipino cane cutters received only 69 cents. The planters constantly reminded the various ethnic groups of their differences in order to divide them. They appealed to the "race pride" of the Filipino laborers to urge them to work as hard as the Japanese laborers. This emphasis on ethnic rivalry led one Filipino work gang leader to declare to his men: "We are all Filipinos, brothers. We all know how to hoe. So, let's do a good job and show the people of other nations what we can do. Let us not shame our skin!"

The planters' divide-and-control plan promoted tensions among the different ethnic groups on the plantations. Sometimes this tension erupted into fistfights in the fields or riots in the camps. On the Spreckelsville Plantation on Maui in 1898, 300 Japanese, wielding sticks and clubs, drove 100 Chinese laborers from the camps. A year later, during a riot between Chinese and Japanese workers on the Kahuku Plantation on Oahu, 60 Chinese were wounded, and four were killed. But the laborers did not only turn their discontent against each other. Most of the time, their rage was aimed at their bosses—and at the whole plantation system.

A mill where cane was processed into sugar for export, mostly to the United States. Working conditions inside the hot, noisy mills were little better than in the fields.

The ditch-man's job was to control the flow of water in the irrigation ditches. Many Chinese and Japanese immigrants were skilled in such work because irrigation had been practiced in their homelands for centuries.

Seasons
of
Rebellion

EVEN IN THE EARLY DAYS OF PLANTATION LABOR, WORK-
ers strove to gain more control over the conditions of their
labor and a greater share of the profits they produced. Instead
of remaining passive, docile, and "childlike," as the managers
wanted them to be, they struggled to improve their lives on
the plantations in many different ways.

Sometimes workers fought back violently, turning
against overseers who physically abused and mistreated them.
Plantation records show many cases of workers assaulting and
beating up cruel and unfair lunas. On a Maui plantation in
1903, for example, after an Irish luna had hit a laborer, he was
attacked by a gang of Chinese workers and buried under a
10-foot pile of cane stalks. The following year, on another
plantation, 200 Korean laborers mobbed the plantation phy-
sician, claiming he had killed a Korean patient with a kick to
the stomach.

On occasion, the workers turned their anger against
property. The dry cane fields were especially easy targets for
arson. In 1899, after police broke up a demonstration of
protesting Chinese laborers on one plantation, a fire swept
through the cane fields.

But while planters worried about violent resistance,
they also had to watch for subtle and ingenious actions. The
very first plantation manager, William Hooper, was the victim
of one particularly clever ruse by his workers. In the 1830s,
Hooper paid his Hawaiian and Chinese workers with coupons—pieces of cardboard upon which he had written
amounts, such as "25 cents" or "50 cents." The workers could

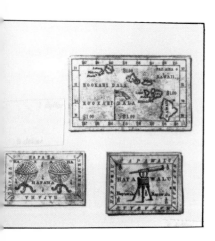

Workers were paid with "tokens," privately printed money for use in the plantation stores. The tokens bore complicated designs so that they could not be counterfeited by ingenious workers.

use the coupons to buy goods at the plantation store. In 1836, Hooper was dismayed to discover that his Hawaiian workers, who had learned how to read and write from a young schoolmaster in the village, were using their new skills to make artful reproductions of his coupons. Soon the Chinese workers were doing it, too. A white neighbor reported that the counterfeits were "so strikingly like the original, imitating the signatures with scrupulous exactness, that it was some time before the fraud was detected."

When he uncovered the deception, Hooper nervously scribbled in his diary, "Some native has attempted to counterfeit the papers which I issued for dollars." In 1839, Hooper sent some of the counterfeit coupons to his company in Honolulu, saying, "I send you up a specimen of what I suppose to be *native* ingenuity in the shape of counterfeit money." He admitted, "I would not swear it was not mine." Hooper asked the company to have currency printed from a copper plate in order to be certain it could not be duplicated, and he gave careful instructions: "If the ground work is fine waved lines, or a delicate net work, and the border highly wrought, we doubt if we shall be troubled with counterfeits from the Chinese or any other source."

But the counterfeit conspiracy was only one episode in a long history of plantation labor struggles. Throughout the islands, workers engaged in day-to-day resistance, working as little as possible. Many of them faked illness in order to get out of working. A visitor to a plantation near Hilo, seeing how many laborers claimed to suffer from certain ailments, said, "It reminds me very much of plantation life in Georgia in the old days of slavery. I never elsewhere heard of so many headaches, sore hands, and other trifling ailments." Like the southern slaves, Hawaii's plantation laborers saw no reason to meet their bosses' demands.

Discipline was a constant problem for the planters, for the laborers had little incentive to work hard. In one of their songs, field hands described their attitude toward work:

When it rains I sleep;
When it's sunny I stay away from work;
And, when cloudy, I spend the day
In drinking wine.

Laborers became skilled at the art of pretending to be working. On the Kohala Plantation, a luna discovered the frustrations of supervising Japanese women in the fields. In his diary, he complained, "It always seemed impossible to keep them together, especially if the fields were not level. The consequence was that these damsels were usually scattered all over the place and as many as possible were out of sight in the gulches or dips in the field where they could not be seen, where they would calmly sit and smoke their little metal pipes until the luna appeared on the skyline, when they would be busy as bees."

To escape from work and daily drudgery, many plantation laborers turned to drugs—opium and alcohol. Visiting a Hilo plantation in 1873, a British traveler named Isabella Bird noted that the Chinese laborers smoked opium. A Chinese plantation worker recalled how the cook would bring their lunches to the field in pails: "In the top of the bucket was a little paper or envelope with the dope in it. All the men took their dope that way with their dinner."

Drinking was also widespread on the plantations. In the Japanese camps on Saturdays, "drinking bouts began everywhere" and an "uproar was made with drinking and singing" until late at night. A Filipino worker remembered how "drinks were readily available because just about everyone knew how to make 'swipe wine.' You just ferment molasses with water and yeast and in a week it's ready. And if you distilled that, you got clear liquor ten times stronger than any gin you could buy from the store."

Planters complained that drinking kept their laborers from doing "anything like a fair day's work." Managers grumbled, "No employees can drink booze and do six honest days' work in a week. They are not 'up to scratch,' even if they can keep awake. . . . Their brains are muddled by booze." After drugging themselves with alcohol on the weekends, laborers were unfit for work on Monday. Inspecting the camps on Mondays, plantation managers sometimes found one-third of their men "dead drunk."

Drugs may have helped the laborers to bear the emptiness they felt on the weekends, as well as the boredom of their meaningless, routine work during the week. Especially in the early years, plantation life offered little entertainment. "There was very little to do when work was over," recalled a Chinese laborer, "and the other fellows who were having a good time smoking asked me to join them, so then in order to be a good sport I took up opium smoking, not realizing that I would probably have to die with it." Another Chinese worker said, "If we don't smoke, we feel as if something were gnawing at our insides. The opium fumes will drive away that feeling and lift us out of our misery into a heaven of blissful rest and peace."

For a short time, drugs let workers escape the reality of the plantation and enter a dream world where they could

In 1900 the Board of Health set fire to Chinatown in Honolulu. A man there was thought to have died of bubonic plague, the dreaded Black Death of the Middle Ages, and panicked public officials thought fire would prevent an epidemic. The fire left 4,000 people homeless.

hear again the voices of fathers, mothers, and other loved ones. Said a Filipino plantation hand, "Drinking killed time and made the work day seem to go faster. At least, it helped feeling like everything was together. So swipe wine was our coffee in the mornings. And swipe was our milk for lunch. Swipe was our evening juice. And swipe was for sleeping. And the next morning again, swipe was for work. Woozy with swipe was the only way I could stay down with patience for work."

But drugs were self-destructive, and they offered only brief pleasure. Some workers sought a more permanent form of escape through desertion. Under the contract labor system, which remained in force until 1900, workers were bound by law to serve their three- to five-year terms. The only way out was to desert. And thousands of contract laborers did flee from their plantations before their contracts ended. A third of all arrests in the years 1890–92 were for desertion.

Planters constantly worried about their contract laborers running away. "On the island of Maui," said an editor of the *Pacific Commercial Advertiser* in 1880, "scarcely a day passes which does not bring along some member of the police force in search of absconding Chinese plantation laborers, who are . . . causing their employers much inconvenience and expense." The diaries of plantation managers are full of references to runaway laborers. One manager's journal contains a list headed "Deserters Japanese." Many of these deserters were repeat offenders:

#5 Nakajin recaught & redeserted
#8 Kaneki
#12 Murohisa recaught & redeserted
#16 Kako
#17 Toshida recaught
#19 Iwamoto
#21 Iamamoto Furokishi
#24 Murakami
#323 Asahare recaught
#326 Hayashi
#400 Imatzu
#418 Saito recaught
#409 Uyeda
#416 Murakami recaught
#655 Nakane
#685 Fukushima Kaisaku recaught
#619 Seto
#621 Kuba recaught Honolulu

The same diary tells the story of a Japanese woman who had abandoned both her boss and her husband: "Ura, wife of Fujinaka #700 deserted on January 1892. Ura was under contract with the K. S. C. [Koloa Sugar Company] to

Sugar was not the only plantation crop. Here rice seedlings are being planted in the mud of a flooded field, or paddy, on Kauai.

50

work for 3 years commencing in May 1891 and therefore was bound to work until May 1894." The luckless Fujinaka not only lost his wife but also had to pay the Koloa Sugar Company because she had deserted.

Although many workers deserted, or tried to, most of them waited until their contracts ended and then left the plantations. In 1859, a newspaper editor reported that many Chinese workers were leaving the plantations at the end of their contracts to join "the crowd of Chinamen already prowling about Honolulu." In January 1882, the manager of a plantation scrawled a worried note in his diary: "Most of our Chinamen gave notice today that they will leave after the end of this month."

By 1882, there were 15,000 Chinese people in Hawaii, but only one-third of them worked on the plantations. Most of them had stayed on the plantations only as long as

A rooming house in Honolulu's Chinatown in 1899. Chinese shops and restaurants multiplied as workers left the plantations to go into business on their own.

A Japanese store in Hawaii. When their labor contracts ended, Japanese workers left the plantations. Many went to the American mainland, but when migration to the mainland was banned in 1907, they made lives for themselves on the islands.

their contracts required. Then they had moved on in search of better jobs. Many became rice farmers, making the swamplands yield rich harvests. Others settled in nearby villages and opened small stores. "My grandfather Len Wai worked on a plantation and operated a store during after-work hours," said Raymond Len. "The store did well and he went full time into it after his contract was up." Most of the discharged Chinese laborers went to Honolulu, where they lived in a bustling Chinatown.

Thousands of Japanese workers also left the plantations after their contracts ended. When the contract labor system was abolished, the workers were no longer bound to the plantations. In the labor camps, Japanese workers eagerly read bulletins and advertisements about higher wages in California, and soon the planters unhappily watched large numbers of their Japanese laborers leaving Hawaii for the

American mainland. To stem this flow, the planters asked Japanese officials in Hawaii to urge the laborers to stay on the plantations. In 1903, the Japanese consul advised his countrymen to "stay at work steadily on the plantations and not go to an uncertainty on the mainland." But the Japanese laborers ignored their consul's advice. They continued to migrate to the mainland in search of the highest bidder for their labor. By 1907, 40,000 Japanese had left Hawaii for the West Coast.

Suddenly, in March of that year, President Theodore Roosevelt issued an order that prevented Hawaii's Japanese from moving to the mainland. Baishiro Tamashiro was one of many Japanese people in Hawaii who had been planning to move to the West Coast. Years later, he vividly remembered his disappointment when he learned about Roosevelt's order: "On March 20th there was a change in the law, and I was prohibited to go to America. It was written all over in the newspapers. We were planning to go on April 9; however, the rule came on the 20th of March. So all my planning was *pau* [Hawaiian for finished]."

At a mass meeting in Honolulu, Japanese laborers angrily denounced Roosevelt's order, saying that it made them permanent slaves of the plantation owners. Frustrated in their desire to leave, trapped in Hawaii by law, the Japanese workers knew they had no choice but to struggle for a better life in the islands.

*Representatives of the 7,000 workers who went on strike in 1909
to protest a pay system that was based on race. Plantation workers
found that the labor strike was their best weapon against unfair
employment practices.*

Chapter Five

Uniting Across Ethnic Barriers

MOST PLANTATION WORKERS REALIZED THAT THE only way they could improve their work and their lives was to act collectively—that is, to work together to benefit everyone. Their most powerful weapon was the strike. They could put down their tools, walk off their jobs, and refuse to work until they had reached an agreement with the managers. But workers also knew that the planters had the power to react brutally to strikes. The past had taught the laborers some harsh lessons.

In 1891, for example, 200 Chinese laborers had gone on strike to protest unfair deductions from their wages. They marched to the courthouse in Kapaau on the island of Hawaii. The plantation managers ordered them to return to their camps, and the strikers left the courthouse late in the afternoon. But as they walked back to the camps, they were confronted by policemen armed with whips. In fear, one or two of the strikers stooped to pick up stones. Suddenly, according to a newspaper report, the Chinese strikers found themselves "in the midst of a general onslaught," and were "ruthlessly overridden and welted with the bullock whips." Pursuing the fleeing strikers, the policemen attacked the Chinese camp, breaking windows and hurling stones. They seized 40 or more Chinese men by their long braids. Some of these victims were seen running in terror, their hair tied to the saddles of galloping horses.

The planters believed they had the right to crush strikes because contract laborers could not legally go on strike. Laborers could be arrested and punished in the courts for refusing to work. But when Hawaii became a U.S. territory in

June 1900 and contract labor was outlawed, the planters could no longer claim that strikes were illegal.

Months before contract labor was officially abolished, plantation workers looked forward to their freedom. In April, Japanese workers in Lahaina went on strike. They were upset because three mill hands had been crushed to death when a sugar pan collapsed. Blaming careless management for the accident, the laborers refused to work. The strikers seized the mill and the town. For 10 days, they defiantly paraded under Japanese flags and even tore down the house of a store clerk who would not give them credit.

The Lahaina strikers were successful. The plantation manager agreed to most of their demands, including a $500 payment to the relatives of each accident victim and a nine-hour day for all workers. Meanwhile, Japanese workers elsewhere had gone on strike. On the Spreckelsville Plantation, they demanded the end of all labor contracts. Two hundred strikers, swinging clubs and throwing stones, fought a posse of 60 policemen and lunas armed with black snake whips. The strikers were "most thoroughly black snaked" and forced to retreat to their camps, but in the end they won. Their labor contracts were canceled.

In 1900, more than 20 strikes swept through the plantations as 8,000 workers stopped working. Although the strikes were led and supported mainly by Japanese workers, two of them involved interethnic cooperation. On the Puehuehu Plantation, Chinese and Japanese laborers struck to protest the withholding of part of their wages (even though their original labor contracts allowed managers to withhold those sums). And on the Kilauea Plantation, Japanese and Portuguese women field hands demanded that their wages be

raised from $8 to $10 a month. Despite management efforts to break the strike, the women stood together and won their wage increases.

After 1900, conflict between managers and workers grew even more intense. Workers found themselves facing the power of the state. In 1906, Japanese workers on the Waipahu Plantation struck for higher wages. Plantation manager E. K. Bull immediately requested police help. Forty-seven police-

Most plantation managers tried to keep workers separated by race and nationality so that they would not form bonds of unity. In this 1899 photograph, German and Portuguese employees are in front, Japanese in the middle, and Chinese in the rear.

men armed with rifles were sent to the plantation, where they served as Bull's private army. The policemen marched on the plantation grounds and patrolled the camps to scare the strikers with a show of force. During a tense moment in the negotiations, Bull threatened to use the police to turn the strikers out of their homes in the camps. Undaunted, the 1,700 Japanese strikers forced Bull to meet some of their demands.

The Waipahu Plantation strike showed the importance of collective labor action. Individual acts of resistance, such as attacking a luna or setting fire to a field, did not seriously weaken the planters' control of the workers and sometimes brought harsh punishment. Drunkenness and phony illnesses were forms of resistance, but they did not change conditions in the workplace. Deserters escaped, but the plantation system remained the same. Strikes, however, could bring about changes for the better—changes that helped *all* workers. The strikes also gave men and women of various nationalities a deeper understanding of themselves as laborers. The strikes made people start to think of themselves as part of the working class, rather than as members of this or that ethnic group.

Crossing the ethnic barriers took time. At first, workers defined their interests in terms of their own ethnic groups. They organized themselves into "blood unions"—labor organizations based on ethnic membership. The Japanese, for example, belonged to the Japanese union, and the Filipinos to the Filipino union.

The most important act of "blood unionism" was the Japanese strike of 1909. Protesting against the racially based wage system, the Japanese strikers demanded higher wages and equal pay for equal work. Angrily they noted that Portuguese laborers were paid $22.50 a month, while Japanese laborers received only $18 a month for the same kind of work. They argued, "If a laborer comes from Japan and he performs the same quantity of work of the same quality within the same period of time as those who hail from the opposite side of the world, what good reason is there to discriminate one as against the other? It is not the color of skin that grows cane in the field. It is labor that grows cane."

The Japanese strikers struggled for four long months. The strike involved 7,000 Japanese plantation laborers on Oahu. Thousands of Japanese workers on the other islands supported the strikers, sending them money and food. Japanese business organizations such as the Honolulu Retail Merchants' Association gave money to the strike fund, and the Japanese Physicians' Association gave free medical service to the strikers and their families. A strong sense of ethnic solidarity inspired the strikers. At rallies, they affirmed their commitment to *yamato damashii*—the spirit of Japan. They told themselves they must "stick together" as Japanese to win the strike.

The strike reflected a new awareness among Japanese workers. They had changed from sojourners who expected to stay in Hawaii for a few years into settlers who hoped to build a future in the islands. They had been transformed from Japanese into Japanese Americans. The strikers explained: "We have decided to permanently settle here . . . to unite our destiny with that of Hawaii, sharing the prosperity and adversity of Hawaii with other citizens of Hawaii." They now had families to support, children to educate, and religious institutions to maintain.

Over time, immigrants from China, Japan, Korea, the Philippines, and elsewhere saw that they had much in common: Work was the thread that bound them together.

Hawaii was becoming home for the Japanese laborers, and they wondered what kind of home it would be. The strikers argued that conditions on the plantations were "undemocratic and un-American." It was not right for wealthy landowners to oppress the workers. This social injustice hurt not only the Japanese workers but everyone in the islands. Fair wages would encourage laborers to work harder, and all of Hawaii would enjoy "perpetual peace and prosperity."

But the planters pressured the government to arrest the Japanese strike leaders for "conspiracy." Then they broke the strike by hiring Korean, Hawaiian, Chinese, and Portuguese laborers as scabs—workers willing to do the jobs of those on strike. The planters also began importing massive numbers of Filipinos to counterbalance the Japanese laborers. The strikers' message was heard, however. Three months later the planters raised the wages of the Japanese workers and stopped paying different wages to workers of different races.

To the Japanese plantation laborers in 1909, an ethnically based strike made good sense. The Japanese made up about 70% of the entire work force, while the Filipinos made up less than 1%. But the ethnic solidarity of the Japanese was also a weakness. Because only the Japanese were on strike, the planters were able to use laborers of other nationalities to break the strike. Eleven years after the strike, only 44% of the work force was Japanese, and 30% was Filipino. Although the Japanese and Filipinos had their own unions at first, they gradually realized that the labor movement needed unity among all members of the working class, regardless of ethnicity. Barriers did exist between Asians of different ethnic backgrounds. Some of those barriers were based on tradition or political events in their homelands, and some had been erected by the planters, who wanted to keep the workers from uniting. Yet as time passed, the barriers began to crumble. An important step toward interethnic unity came in 1920.

In December 1919, the Japanese Federation of Labor and the Filipino Federation of Labor made separate demands to the Hawaiian Sugar Planters' Association. The workers wanted higher wages, an eight-hour day, insurance for elderly retired employees, and paid maternity leave. Both sets of demands were promptly turned down by the planters.

The Japanese Federation of Labor asked the managers to reconsider their decision. The Japanese labor leaders

61

wanted to try peaceful methods first. They believed the labor unions should not act rashly. They urged both unions to prepare for a long strike and plan a successful strategy.

The Filipino Federation of Labor, however, felt that the time had come for action. In January 1920, Pablo Manlapit, head of the Filipino union, told the Filipinos to strike. He urged the Japanese to join them. In his appeal to the Japanese Federation of Labor, Manlapit eloquently called for interethnic working class solidarity: "This is the opportunity that the Japanese should grasp, to show that they are in harmony with and willing to cooperate with other nationalities in this territory, concerning the principles of organized labor. . . . We should work on this strike shoulder to shoulder."

Meanwhile, 3,000 Filipino workers on Oahu's plantations went out on strike. They called upon the Japanese laborers to join them. "What's the matter? Why you hanahana [work]?" the Filipino strikers asked their Japanese co-workers. Several Japanese newspapers urged cooperation with the striking Filipinos. One paper scolded Japanese workers for their hesitation in joining the Filipinos, saying, "Our sincere and desperate voices are also their voices. Their righteous indignation is our righteous indignation. . . . Fellow Japanese laborers! Don't be a race of unreliable dishonest people! Their problem is your problem!" Another Japanese paper declared that between Filipinos and Japanese there should be "no barriers of nationality, race, or color."

A week after the Filipino strike began, the Japanese Federation of Labor ordered its members to strike. United in struggle, 8,300 Filipino and Japanese strikers—77% of the entire plantation work force on Oahu—brought plantation operations to a halt. "Pau hana," they told each other, "no go work." "Pau hana," they declared defiantly, "we on strike."

Determined to break the strike, planters quickly turned to their divide-and-control strategy. One owner told a plantation manager, "We are inclined to think that the best prospect, in connection with this strike, is the fact that two organizations, not entirely in harmony with each other, are connected with it, and if either of them falls out of line, the end will be in sight."

The planters drove a wedge between the Filipino and Japanese leaders. They offered a bribe to Manlapit, the Fili-

A strikers' parade in 1920. Although the 1919–20 strike ended in defeat for the workers, it proved that people of different ethnic backgrounds could join together for the common good.

The Salvation Army and labor cooperatives provided means and shelter for the 12,000 people who were evicted from their homes on the plantations during the 1919–20 strike by Japanese and Filipino workers. The seven-month strike cost the plantations an estimated $12 million.

pino leader—and suddenly, to the surprise of both the Filipino and Japanese strikers, Manlapit called off the strike, saying it was a Japanese plot to cripple Hawaiian industry. But in spite of Manlapit's reversal, many Filipinos remained on strike with the Japanese. The planters stepped up their attack, saying that the strikers were puppets of Japan who planned to "Japanise" the islands.

The planters also took direct action to break the strike. They enlisted Hawaiians, Portuguese, and Koreans as strikebreakers. The planters knew that Koreans had a particular enmity for the Japanese because Japan had invaded Korea a few years earlier. For this reason, they often used Koreans to help break Japanese strikes. During the 1920 strike, Korean laborers under the leadership of the Korean National Association announced, "We place ourselves irrevocably against the Japanese and the present strike. We don't wish to be looked upon as strikebreakers, but we shall continue to work . . . and we are opposed to the Japanese in everything." More than 100 Korean men and women organized themselves into a Strikebreakers' Association and offered their services to the Hawaiian Sugar Planters' Association.

The planters also sent eviction notices to the striking workers, forcing them to leave their homes within 48 hours. The workers and their families sought shelter in empty lots in Honolulu. At the time, an epidemic of influenza was raging in many parts of the world, including Hawaii. Crowded into makeshift shelters during the height of the epidemic, thousands of strikers and their family members fell ill, and 150 of them died. "My brother and mother had a high fever," Tadao Okada recalled, "but all of us were kicked out of our home." Under such punishing and chaotic conditions, the strikers could not hold out forever. They called off the strike in July.

But although they were soundly beaten, the workers had learned a valuable lesson from the 1920 strike. Filipinos and Japanese, joined by Spanish, Portuguese, and Chinese laborers, had shared the first major interethnic working-class struggle in Hawaii. Men and women of different backgrounds had realized that the same whistle woke all of them at five A.M., and that they sweated together all day in the same fields and mills. They had united to fight for a common goal. And as they walked the picket lines and protested at mass rallies together, they came to understand how their years of work had turned Hawaii into a wealthy and profitable place. "When we first came to Hawaii," they proudly declared, "these islands were covered with ohia forests, guava fields and areas of wild grass. Day and night did we work, cutting trees and burning grass, clearing lands and cultivating fields until we made the plantations what they are today."

During the strike, as the workers reached across ethnic boundaries for a new unity, the Japanese labor leaders questioned the need for two separate unions, one for the Japanese and one for the Filipinos. Suggesting that the two federations could be merged into one union, they insisted that Japanese workers must link themselves with people of other nationalities. All of them were laborers, and they should work together to safeguard their standard of living. So, in the middle of the strike, the Japanese Federation of Labor was transformed into an interracial union called the Hawaii Laborers' Association—a name that spoke of solidarity among *all* workers.

A leader of the Hawaii Laborers' Association described this new view of the working class. Japanese and Filipinos had acted in "a solid body" during the strike, said Takashi Tsutsumi. From their struggle, the workers had learned they needed "a big, powerful and non-racial labor organization" that would bring together "laborers of all nationalities."

The 1920 strike had provided a vision, a basis for a new union. For the first time, large numbers of workers had crossed ethnic barriers to cooperate against the planter class. "This is the feature that distinguishes the recent movement from all others," Tsutsumi observed. He predicted that a large, interracial union would emerge within 10 years, springing from a "Hawaiian-born" leadership. "When that day comes," he said, "the strike of 1920 would surely be looked upon as most significant."

The idea of unity across ethnic lines fired the imagination of Milton Murayama, the son of a plantation laborer, who became a writer. In his novel *All I Asking for Is My Body,* Murayama describes an incident on a Maui plantation. During a strike of Filipino workers, the manager tries to recruit Japanese boys as scabs. The boys are glad to make some extra money. Then they begin talking about the strike at school.

"What's freedom?" asks Tubby Takeshita, and the teacher and students agree that freedom means being your "own boss," not "part of a pecking order." They soon realize that workers are at the bottom of the pecking order and getting a "raw deal." "You gotta stick together even more if you the underdog," Tubby says. And the teacher asks: "How much together? Filipino labor, period? Japanese labor, period? Or all labor?" A union of "all labor" had not yet been achieved in Hawaii, but the strike of 1920 had paved the way.

In the early days, immigrants arrived to find that their new homes in the plantation were nothing more than huts or sheds.

Chapter Six

Life
in the
Plantation
Camps

MILTON MURAYAMA'S NOVEL *ALL I ASKING FOR IS MY BODY* gives a vivid picture of how the different classes of people on the plantation lived. At the top of the hill was the big house, the luxurious home of the manager. Below this were the nice-looking homes of the Portuguese, Spanish, and Japanese lunas. Next came the identical wooden-frame houses of Japanese Camp; lower still was the more run-down Filipino Camp. Through each level ran the concrete sewage ditches that drained the toilets and outhouses of the levels above.

The houses reflected the strict social ranking of the plantation community. The manager lived in a mansion with spacious verandas and white columns overlooking the plantation. His foremen and the technical employees were housed in handsome bungalow cottages, surrounded by well-kept lawns and flower gardens. "This section of houses on this tree-lined street is called 'lunas row,'" my cousin Minoru Takaki pointed out as he drove me around the Puunene Plantation on Maui in 1985. "Only the white lunas could live here, in the nice houses." As we passed a recreational hall, he said, "That's 'haole club.' In the old days, only haoles were allowed to go there. It was segregated." Then he chuckled, "But you know what, my mother could go there. She was the maid."

A government inspector found that the kind of housing on the plantations varied according to race. European families received two rooms, and single European men received one room in a four-room cottage. But Chinese workers were placed in barracks where each room was shared by anywhere from six to forty men.

Workers of different nationalities were usually housed in separate camps. "There were the Japanese camps," said my uncle Richard Okawa, describing the Hawi Plantation on the Big Island, "and the Chinese and Filipino camps, and one camp for the Puerto Ricans. Our family used to sell fish on the side, and your mother and I when we were young kids had to go from camp to camp on pay day and collect the money the workers owed for the fish." The Puunene Plantation on Maui had 16 camps, including many Japanese and Filipino camps as well as two Chinese camps, two Spanish camps, and "Alabama Camp," where black workers lived.

This ethnic and racial segregation came about because the planters had imported workers from different countries at different times. As each new group arrived, a new camp was built. From the planters' point of view, this segregated arrangement was good. It helped keep the various ethnic groups apart so that they would not form unions.

But the ethnically separated camps were not just a device to control the workers. Most of the workers *wanted* to live in segregated camps. Their new lives in Hawaii seemed less strange and forbidding when they were surrounded by people like themselves, lulled by familiar accents. They could practice the customs and traditions of their homelands and speak their native languages.

A Filipino worker on the Ewa Plantation explained that at first all of the workers lived in one camp: "There were Puerto Ricans, Spanish, a handful of Portuguese, Chinese, a few Japanese and a few Koreans. Each nationality group more or less constituted an exclusive group of its own; no group seemed to mingle with any other. . . . Every year there were many Filipino immigrants who joined our camp. There were so many Filipinos that a separate camp was given to them. The other nationalities soon had a camp of their own too, a thing which pleased everyone, as not only work was thought of but also parties among the laborers could be held."

Not all of the plantations had separate ethnic camps. On a few plantations, managers deliberately integrated the camps. On the Waialua Plantation, for example, the first Korean workers were placed in a separate camp right after they arrived in 1903, to avoid the "danger of race troubles of any kind with Japanese, Chinese or Portuguese." Later they would be merged into the "regular plantation camps." The manager explained that after they mingled with other workers, the Koreans would "lose their identity as Koreans and be merged into the plantation community as a whole."

Describing one of the camps on the Waipahu Plantation, a Japanese laborer said, "In those days, we were living in a part of Waipahu called Pake [Chinese] Camp. In that camp, Pake and Japanese were all mixed up. We didn't have any trouble with the Pake." A book published in 1924 praised the integrated camps of the Hawaiian Commercial and Sugar Company on Maui, saying, "None of the camps are given over to one race exclusively, and equal treatment is given to all. The result of this mixing of all races in one village has been the disappearance of racial antagonisms and jealousies and the development of mutual respect." According to this writer, the integration of workers helped create tolerant communities, free of prejudice.

The condition of the camps varied from plantation to plantation. In 1899, an inspector for the Bureau of Immigration found some model camps with weatherproof houses and clean yards. But he also visited run-down, ramshackle camps

71

Japanese workers at a plantation camp in 1885, four years after the start of emigration from Japan. Over the years to come, crude camps like this one would be transformed into family communities.

"with roofs leaking and danger and disease threatening the occupants." Seventeen years later, another investigator also reported a wide range of housing conditions. Some plantations had "splendid camps," "very clean" and "well-planted" with flowers. But other plantations had very dirty camps with houses in "a rotten condition."

Most plantation laborers lived in crowded and unsanitary camps. One Japanese worker compared the houses to overcrowded pig sties. Another recalled that 50 people, both single men and married couples, shared a long, 10-foot-wide shed with a grass floor. A woman described the "large partitioned house" where she lived: "The type of room for married people was small, no bed or anything." There was just room for a mattress on the floor, a single wicker trunk to hold their possessions, and a nail on which to hang their clothes.

Chinese laborers on the Paia Plantation were crowded into "big warehouses filled with bunks stacked four or five high, steamer style. Two or three hundred lived in a building." A Korean visitor found Korean workers living in cramped and dirty conditions: "The married men each occupy one room, but single ones are put in compartments in groups of five or six people. The filth and uncleanliness of their living quarters are beyond description." In many instances, six men occupied a small 8-by-12-foot room; two families had to share a single room. The lack of privacy and space made the workers tense and nervous. "Ten of us shared a small house and in such a cramped space we were constantly brushing against each other," a Filipino worker said. "We were often irritated at each other. Small annoyances led to quarrels. Endless arguments arose as to whose turn it was to prepare supper, wash dishes or buy the food. An innocent remark or comment, interpreted wrongly, might result in a fight."

When workers went on strike, they often protested against the poor condition of the camps. After the Japanese strike of 1909, planters admitted that they needed to improve the camps. In 1910, the Hawaiian Sugar Planters' Association advised planters to award cash prizes to workers who had the prettiest yards and gardens. This would encourage workers to clean up their camps and take care of them. But the association was not actually concerned with the well-being of the workers. It just wanted the planters and the plantations to look good

A plantation barber at work. The camps were self-sufficient communities in which people found most of the goods and services they needed. Workers seldom left the plantation.

to visitors from outside. "An attractive camp," the association stated, "is something which always attracts visitors, and which always gives them a favorable impression of the treatment of laborers by the plantations."

The planters also knew that improving the camps was in their own best interests. If the camps were clean and comfortable, the workers who lived in them would be happier—and would work harder. "Pleasant surroundings, with some of the modern comforts and conveniences," explained a plantation official, "go a long way to make the worker healthier and more efficient in his work."

At first, most of the Asian plantation workers were single men who were housed in barracks. But when planters began hiring men with families rather than single men, they started building cottages for families. Planters preferred married men with families because they thought that married men were more reliable, less likely to run away or get drunk than single men. One labor supplier explained in 1916 that "dependable married men" made better workers and that families should have their own cottages to live in. In 1920, the Hawaiian Sugar Planters' Association reported, "Housing conditions on the plantations have changed greatly during the past few years" because of the switch from single to married workers.

The laborers had their own reasons for beautifying their camps. Seeking to add a small bit of beauty and a reminder of their homeland, Japanese workers placed bonsai plants—tiny, carefully nurtured trees—on the steps of their cottages. They also created artistic gardens. One visitor from the mainland said that the flowers and "miniature gardens with little rocky pools and goldfish" were like "a corner of Japan."

Workers grew vegetables on garden plots assigned to them by the plantation manager. One plantation official described an extensive system of vegetable gardens: "Each family is given a plot . . . and given water for the purpose of irrigation. These gardens have been very successful and supply a large part of the vegetable need of the family." A Japanese laborer recalled how he cultivated his garden even after 10 hours of hard work in the cane fields. "After we came home from the field," he said, "it was dark especially in the winter months but we tilled our little vegetable garden with the help of the kerosene lamp light to raise the vegetables we ate."

Over the years, the workers changed the camps from collections of impersonal barracks into communities for families. As they landscaped their yards and planted vegetable gardens, they developed a "home feeling." People in the camps began to know and care for each other. In Milton Murayama's novel about plantation life, a character named Kiyoshi says, "There was another thing I'd come to like about the camp. The hundred Japanese families were like one big family. Everybody knew everybody else, everybody was friendly."

Still, most of the time plantation life was isolated and drab. "For the first two and a half years here," a Filipino worker recounted, "I lived pretty much the same. Six days a week I worked from siren to siren." To escape from the plantation routine, laborers found ways to entertain themselves. Many of them went fishing. A Filipino worker said that he "went with friends to the rocky edge of the ocean" to fish on Sundays.

Ethnic arts and customs remained alive on the plantations. These traveling Japanese musicians went from camp to camp, entertaining workers and their families with familiar songs.

Lonely, far away from families they had left behind in their homelands, many workers sought entertainment by playing cards and gambling. "Here and there gambling was in favor," recalled a Japanese man. "On the Saturday evening following pay day, questionable women and professional gamblers from Honolulu came on business to the camp. . . . And the visitors wrung from the workers the fruits of their painstaking toil." Chinese gamblers traveled from plantation to plantation, and gambling in the Chinese camps became so

intense that it sometimes interfered with work. In 1881, an annoyed plantation manager wrote in his diary that there were "only a few Chinamen carrying cane"—the rest were gambling or watching the games. He sent a foreman to drive the gamblers off the plantation.

A few years later, the Japanese consul reported that gambling among Japanese workers had reached a point where "all night sessions" were "common." A Japanese laborer named Baishiro Tamashiro became so involved in gambling that he stopped working. "When I won, I would pay for my cook charge first of all," he recalled. "If not, I had to borrow money. I spent about half a year on gambling."

Many workers spent their weekends and nights gambling to help them forget their hardships. They hoped to win big; perhaps they could even win enough money to return home rich. Usually, however, they lost. In the fields the next day, they would sing:

> *The thirty-five cents*
> *That I earned and saved*
> *Is gone by night*
> *From gambling.*

Many Filipino laborers found their wages gone by the end of the evening, spent at dance halls. There were few Filipino women on the plantations, and Filipino men crowded the dance halls, craving the company of women. They eagerly purchased tickets that offered them momentary joy: For each ticket, they could dance with a woman for three minutes. "Some guys, they spend $50, $30, one man, one night," recalled a musician who played in the dance halls. "Go for broke, the men."

77

After the 1909 strike, planters saw that they needed to provide recreation for their workers. The Hawaiian Sugar Planters' Association advised managers to offer amusements on the plantations. A "welfare program" of sports, music, and movies, said a sugar industry official, would bring "magnificent results." Recreation would hold laborers on the plantations, and it would also help prevent strikes. In short, a recreational program would not only be good for the workers but it would also be good for business.

The association suggested that planters should provide movies, baseball fields, and instruments for workers' bands and orchestras. Nine years later, a plantation manager reported on the good effects of his recreation program: "Every Sunday we have baseball games between the Filipino laborers and our young Japanese and Portuguese boys in which our timekeepers and some of our overseers join. . . . In looking around at the almost universal unrest amongst labor and thinking of the absence of it upon these Islands, we feel that an unremitting endeavor should be made to keep our laborers content and happy."

Religion, too, was part of plantation life. The planters supported their laborers' religious activities. Some Chinese workers came to Hawaii as Christians, baptized by Lutheran missionaries in China. Others adopted Christianity in Hawaii, where missionaries were busy preaching Christianity to both the native Hawaiian people and the migrants from Asia. Chinese plantation laborers were given Chinese translations of the Bible, and the missionaries and planters encouraged them to form congregations of Chinese Christians.

One of the most energetic Chinese Christians was S. P. Aheong, who arrived on Maui in 1854 as a contract

laborer. A missionary converted him to Christianity, and then he took up missionary work himself. He traveled from island to island, visiting plantations and holding religious meetings for his fellow Chinese. During his first 10 months of religious work, he gave 75 sermons in Chinese. A letter he wrote in 1868 describes one of these services. "Five out of 13 Chinamen came," Aheong wrote. "I gave them some books to read which know how to read. One of them says how can a man say that China's idols are not the God because if a man say a bad word to the idol, then he shall have pain in the whole body. I say to him that he has by all mistaking, for I am since the great many years refuse the idol; and speak bad word to them but I do not pain my body at all, and I told him good deal about our heavenly father is the true God." A few weeks later, Aheong wrote of his fellow Chinese migrants, "Some of them been in this country more than 40 or 30 years, and never

A Japanese baseball team in Honolulu in 1904. Plantation managers introduced sports, especially baseball, to the plantations to make workers more satisfied with their lives.

79

been to church since they been in these Islands, until I came here."

But it was the Koreans who made Christianity a strong presence on the plantations. Many of them had become Christians in Korea. They built plantation churches shortly after their arrival in Hawaii. A missionary who visited several plantations in 1905 said that seven chapels were being built for Koreans. "A good part of the money," he noted, "was subscribed by the plantation proprietors who are keen to encourage all agencies looking toward peace and order and

A Filipino church celebrates its fifth anniversary in 1920. Churches and temples were an important part of camp life.

morality." Planters regarded their support for Korean churches as a "paying investment." One planter declared that the Korean Christians were his "most desirable and efficient laborers."

Christianity spread rapidly among the Koreans in Hawaii. In 1906 a visiting missionary was delighted to find "little congregations" of worshiping Koreans everywhere in the islands. "In the evening," he reported, "the sound of their hymns can be heard in most camps." He estimated that one-third of all the Koreans in Hawaii were Christians, and he approved of the way they helped stamp out gambling and drunkenness in the camps.

Buddhism, a faith that had flourished in Japan for centuries, traveled to Hawaii with the Japanese labor migrants. On every plantation, the Japanese built Buddhist temples. The planters often donated land for the temples and even paid for Buddhist programs and priests, for they believed that Buddhism helped make the workers more orderly and settled. In 1902, a sugar industry director encouraged planters to give financial aid to Japanese Buddhist schools and added, "The Directors are quite in sympathy with any movement on the part of the Japanese which should have good influence amongst them." Religion, like baseball games and better housing, served the needs of both workers and planters.

The workers, much more than the planters, ultimately defined the quality of camp life. Through small individual efforts such as planting gardens, and through large collective efforts such as founding churches, they built communities where only rows of impersonal barracks had stood. Within these communities, each group of immigrants cherished memories and traditions of its own Asian homeland.

A young Japanese girl and her baby brother. When they began to raise families in Hawaii, the Asian immigrants changed from temporary sojourners to settlers who planned a future for their children in the new land.

Chapter Seven

A Multicultural Mosaic

ALTHOUGH THEY SERVED THE SPIRITUAL NEEDS OF the workers, the churches and temples that sprang up on plantations also filled another deep urge—the need for ethnic identity. Separated from their homelands by thousands of miles of ocean, workers strove to retain their national identities. In the camps, they celebrated their traditional festivals, recapturing familiar scenes from the old countries.

One of the noisiest and most colorful festivals was Chinese New Year. "The explosion of fire crackers throughout the day," reported the *Hawaiian Gazette* in 1867, "demonstrated that the great day of the Chinese year was being properly remembered." On their New Year's Day, usually in February, Chinese plantation laborers had a holiday. They trimmed their roofs with "long lines of small flags of every hue," and they hung colored lanterns on the porches of their barracks and cottages. Then they exchanged cards or slips of paper to wish each other good luck. Music from Chinese stringed instruments filled the air. The highlight of one traveler's visit to a plantation in 1888 was the Chinese New Year's festival, enlivened with the "tremendous cracking and fizzing" of many firecrackers. During festival time on the Kohala Plantation, two Chinese societies competed to see which could burn the longest or loudest string of firecrackers.

During the midsummer, Japanese plantation laborers held their traditional *obon*, or festival of souls. Dressed in kimonos, they danced in circles to the beat of drums, celebrating the reunion of the living with the spirits of the dead. In early November, they observed the emperor's birthday as a holiday. Plantation managers were irritated by this interrup-

Flags and kites decorate the camp for Boys' Day, a Japanese holiday. Chinese, Korean, and Filipino workers also celebrated their ethnic holidays in traditional ways.

tion of the work schedule, but they had no choice but to give their Japanese workers the day off. Japanese worker Tokusuke Oshiro recalled, "The Emperor's Birthday was celebrated everywhere. Mainly there was *sumo* [wrestling]. . . . Several young men, usually the good ones, got together at a camp and had Japanese-style *sumo* matches." Another migrant said that on the emperor's birthday, workers "would rest from work" and order special lunches. At night they danced to the music of *shamisens*, traditional Japanese stringed instruments, that they had made from tin cans.

The most important celebration for the Filipino plantation laborers was Rizal Day, December 30. On that date in 1896, José Rizal, a Filipino revolutionary leader, was executed by the Spanish rulers of the Philippines. To honor Rizal, Filipino plantation bands played mandolins and guitars at outdoor concerts. Filipino laborers told each other tales of Rizal's heroic deeds. "The Kastilas [Spanish] could not kill him, because the bullets bounced off his chest," a worker would declare. And a friend would "tell it up one notch" by adding that Rizal caught the bullets "with his bare hands!" Over and over, Filipinos told the story about how Rizal had not really died: "After he was buried, his wife poured his love potion on his freshly filled grave, and in the night—he rose, Rizal rose from the grave."

Festivals and myths were not the only pieces of home that the Asian plantation workers carried to Hawaii. They also brought their foods. The camps offered a delicious and unique array of Asian ethnic foods: Chinese *char siu* (barbecued pork) and *bao* (buns with pork stuffing); Korean kimchi (pickled cabbage with garlic and hot red pepper); Filipino adobo (stewed garlic pork and chicken); Japanese sashimi (raw fish) and sushi (rice cakes with seafood). A Japanese specialty called tofu, soybean curd, was in great demand on the plantations. Japanese families also made *mochi* (sweet rice cakes), especially on New Year's Day.

As the laborers and their families mingled together in the camps, they began to share their different foods—not only Asian dishes but also Hawaiian *kalua* pig (baked in the ground) and *lau lau* (fish and pork wrapped in banana leaves) and Portuguese sausage and sweet bread. The daughter of a Portuguese laborer remembered how her mother had made gifts of bread and "little buns for the children in the camp. The Japanese families gave us sushis and the Hawaiians would give us fish." Crossing ethnic lines, workers would taste each other's foods and exclaim in Hawaiian, "*Ono, ono!*" —"Tasty, tasty!"

Sitting on the ground in the cane fields, sharing their lunches, workers of different nationalities also began talking to each other. At first, each person spoke only his or her native

Sumo wrestling, a traditional Japanese sport, attracted crowds in the Japanese camps.

language. Language gave each ethnic group a sense of community within the plantation camps. Talking together in familiar words and phrases, people created ties with each other as they shared memories of their distant homeland and stories of their experiences in the new country. Many parents thought it was important for their children to learn the language of the old country. Japanese and Korean parents sent their children to language schools. After spending the day at public school, a Japanese child would spend another hour or two in Japanese school, and a Korean child would attend Korean school.

Gradually, however, workers of different nationalities began to acquire a common language. In order to work together, they had to communicate across ethnic lines. They also had to understand the plantation managers, who spoke English. Managers wanted the immigrant laborers to be taught a simple form of spoken English. "By this," explained a planter, "we do not mean the English of Shakespeare but the terms used in everyday plantation life. A great many of the small troubles arise from the imperfect understanding between overseers and laborers."

A type of "pidgin English" developed on the plantations. It used bits and pieces from many languages, including English, Hawaiian, Japanese, Portuguese, and Chinese. A foreman could give instructions to an ethnically diverse gang of workers in pidgin English. This allowed the foreman to communicate to all of the workers at once, rather than translating each order into several different languages. In turn, workers could respond to their overseers in pidgin English, and they could also use it to communicate with fellow workers from other countries.

Isolated on the plantations, workers sometimes came to think pidgin *was* the English language. On one occasion, Chinese workers found they could not understand their new white field boss, a haole who had just arrived in Hawaii. He gave his instructions to the men in "pure English," telling them to cut the cane close to the ground, cut the tops off the stalks, and throw the tops between the furrows for fertilizer. But his men found his English strange; they could not understand him. A bystander noticed the confusion and gave the orders in pidgin:

> *Luna,* big boss speak, all men down below cutch; suppose too much *mauka* (uphill, high) cutch, too mucha sugar *poho* (wasted)—*keiki* (shoots) no use. Savvy? (Do you understand?) All men *opala* (trash) cutch, one side t'row—byenby mule men come, *lepo* (dirt) too mucha guru (good). Savvy" "Savvy," the Chinese men replied and added in disgust: "Huy! wasamalla dis *Haole*—he no can taok *haole!*"

A Japanese worker later recalled, "Our English in those days was really funny. A contract worker in Lahaina Plantation was asked by his superiors, 'How many people are working here?' He answered, 'Ten, ten, wan burooku' (Ten, ten, one broke), in loud voice. . . . What the worker meant to say is that ten plus ten minus one, 19."

The workers happily combined words from different languages. The question, "Will you pick coffee?" became "You like hemo coppe ka?" *Hemo* was Hawaiian; *coppe ka* was Japanese. "Chicken he too much makee" meant "Many chickens died"; *makee* was a Hawaiian word. Workers also invented their own expressions such as "mo betta": "Cow he mo betta come home." Newspapers even carried advertisements in pidgin English, such as this announcement of the opening of a new Chinese restaurant on Hotel Street:

> Me—P. Y. Chong plenty smile any time now. Anybody too muchee kokua Me—P. Y. Chong new chop sui lestlunt fix up Hotel Stleet between Nuuanu and Smith. Too many person come Hotel Stleet Lau Yee Chai, catchem Me—P. Y. Chong Numbeh One kaukau lunch time, dinneah time, afteh-theateh suppeh time, any time catchem. Disee new Lau Yee Chai chop sui place no so hard to find, Chinee red and Chinee jade paint all oveh. Numbeh One lestlunt, no so muchee money cost kaukau. You come looksee, eh? Me—P. Y. Chong tank you so muchee.

Lunas and workers mixed Japanese and Hawaiian words with hand gestures. A Japanese worker said, "The Portuguese luna used to speak a little Japanese . . . and the luna would pantomime with his hands and feet what we were supposed to do. We somehow managed to communicate." In the process of giving and receiving orders, the lunas and workers created a new language of lilting phrases and expressive gestures.

As pidgin English became the common language in the camps, it gave people a new identity—one that was associated with Hawaii rather than with Asia. A Korean mother remembered noticing that her children were growing up as "Hawaiians," for they spoke "Hawaiian English" much more fluently than their native tongue. When they spoke pidgin English, the immigrants and their children were no longer purely Chinese, Japanese, Korean, or Filipino. They were developing a Hawaiian identity that was shared by all.

By transplanting their customs and traditions and foods to the camps, building new churches and temples, and creating the new language of pidgin English, the Asian immigrants created a new and distinctive community. The world of plantation Hawaii was like a mosaic, a large picture made of many tiny bits of different-colored stone or glass. In Hawaii, people and elements from many backgrounds came together to form a pattern. Just as each bit of stone or glass shines with its own color, each ethnic group retained its unique qualities, but together they formed something new: a multicultural mosaic.

A plantation school. Education made many workers' children eager to escape the plantation. They were determined to have better lives than their parents had.

Asian women made significant contributions to the economic life of Hawaii. Not only did they work on plantations, but many operated businesses. A majority of early gas stations were run by Japanese women.

Chapter Eight

New Futures

AS WORKERS FROM DIFFERENT ASIAN COUNTRIES learned to share a common language, pidgin English, they found themselves developing a new outlook toward themselves and toward Hawaii. At first, most of the Asian laborers came to the islands as sojourners, planning to earn money and then return to their homelands. In the end, however, many of them settled in Hawaii.

Between 1852 and 1887, for example, 26,000 Chinese arrived in the islands. Only 38% of them went back to China. Of the 200,000 Japanese who came to Hawaii between 1885 and 1924, 55% returned to Japan. Between 1903 and 1910, 7,300 Koreans migrated to Hawaii, but only 16% of them saw their homeland again. And of the 112,800 Filipinos who came to the islands between 1909 and 1931, only 36% returned to the Philippines.

As the years passed, the Asian immigrants found themselves establishing families in the new land. The first arrivals were men, but gradually they were joined by women. Many planters, preferring married workers to single men, encouraged women and families to immigrate. By 1930, nearly 40% of the Chinese population in Hawaii was female. Marriages also occurred between Chinese men and Hawaiian women. In 1900, about 1,500 Chinese men were married to or living with Hawaiian women. Their children were the first Chinese-Hawaiian generation.

Some Chinese men had two families. They were married to Hawaiian women in the islands, but they also had Chinese wives in the old country. Len Wai, for example, left his wife Len Mau Nin in China when he sailed to Hawaii as

91

a contract laborer in 1882. "Every seven years after his initial arrival in the islands," reported his grandson Raymond Len, "he returned to China. My uncle was born there in 1889, my auntie in 1896, and my father, Len Too Shing, in 1903. While in Hawaii, my grandfather also had an Hawaiian wife and they adopted two Hawaiian children." When Raymond Len's father came to the islands, he became part of this Chinese-Hawaiian family. He spoke to his father in Chinese and to his "new Hawaiian mother" in Hawaiian. Asked whether he saw himself as Chinese or Hawaiian, Len Too Shing replied, "I didn't think of myself as anything. I was just a 'local' kid." His Hawaiian mother died in 1930. Two years later, 50 years after first arriving in Hawaii, his father returned to his wife in China.

Chinese-Hawaiian children who had been born in Hawaii were sometimes taken to China. A Chinese-Hawaiian man remembered how he had accompanied his father to China when he was eight years old. That was when he discovered he had "two mothers." His father's Chinese wife treated him "just like her own son." "Hawaiian mother good too, treat me good," he said, "but China mother very, very good."

A few Chinese men took their Hawaiian wives to China. Other men eventually brought their Chinese wives to the islands, where they maintained both their "Chinese family" and their "Hawaiian family." In Chinese-Hawaiian families, languages, customs, and foods were "mixed." The daughter of one such family said, "When my mother just married my father she didn't know any Chinese. Later she picked up Chinese and now she can speak enough to carry on conversation. She speaks Chinese to our Chinese relatives and friends. My father speaks Chinese mostly, but some Hawaiian.

We have a mixture of food at home. . . . Every time we have Hawaiian food we also have rice and other cooked vegetables."

Families were also forming among the other Asian groups as women arrived from the homelands. By 1920, 46% of the Japanese and 30% of the Koreans in Hawaii were women. Women and children accounted for 19% of all Filipino immigrants between 1909 and 1924. A new generation of Asian Americans was taking root in Hawaii, and the islands were becoming home. A plantation work song expressed the new sense of belonging:

> *With one woven basket*
> *Alone I came*
> *Now I have children*
> *And even grandchildren too.*

Sojourners when they arrived in the islands, the immigrant plantation laborers gradually found themselves becoming settlers. My grandparents Kasuke and Katsu Okawa had eight children who were born in Hawaii. In 1922, they

The Takaki family on a Maui plantation in 1919. My grandfather is seated; my father is standing at the far right.

left the Hawi Plantation on the Big Island and bought a house in Honolulu. Another Japanese immigrant, Asakichi Inouye, wrote to his brother in Japan, explaining why he had decided not to return there: "My children are here, and my grandson, and it is here that I have passed most of the days of my life. I do not believe that my wife and I, in our last years, could find contentment in Yokoyama, which has become for us a strange place." In his autobiographical novel *Hawaii: End of the Rainbow*, Kazuo Miyamoto told of the decision to stay in the new land:

> With the passage of the years, he came to love Kauai as a place to live and possibly raise a family. The carefree atmosphere of this new country, not tied down by century-old traditions and taboos, and an immense opportunity that existed for those that could settle and seek their fortune, changed Seikichi's original intention of returning to this homeland at the expiration of the three year contract.

A second-generation Korean, born on a plantation in 1905, told a similar story: "My parents . . . left Korea in the early part of 1903 and came to the Hawaiian Islands. Their intention was to return to their land as soon as they had saved money. In this hope they were disappointed, for they soon found out that it was not so easy to save money as they thought it would be. However, they became so used to the climate, freedom and advantages of this land that they no longer desired to leave this land permanently."

When Shokichi and Matsu Fukuda emigrated from Japan to Maui in 1900, they were sojourners, not planning to stay in Hawaii. In fact, they left their six-month-old baby,

Fusayo, with her grandparents. Some twenty years later, after Fusayo herself had emigrated to California, they decided to return to Japan, taking their Hawaiian-born children with them. But their son Minoru was a teenager by then, and Hawaii was his home, the only world he knew and loved. "He refused to go," remembered his niece. "Japan was a foreign country to him. He was very adamant that the family should stay in Hawaii."

My aunt Mitsue Takaki also found herself planting new roots in Hawaii. She had come to Hawaii in 1920 to marry my uncle Teizo; eleven years later, Teizo injured his knee at work and returned to Japan for medical treatment. When he tried to get back into Hawaii, the immigration authorities refused to let him enter. Mitsue chose to remain in the islands with her three small children, Minoru, Susumu, and Kimiyo. She went to night school to learn English and worked on the Puunene Plantation to support her children. She wanted them to be educated and have opportunities in the land of their birth.

But the planters did not want the children of immigrant workers to advance themselves through education. Planters needed the second generation as laborers. Furthermore, they viewed Asians as a racially subordinate labor class that should not have opportunities outside of the plantation. The planters' children were expected to be planters—and the laborers' children were expected to be laborers. In 1928, several white boys at an elite high school for the children of the planter class were asked to talk about their career plans. "What do we care about these vocational discussions?" one of them snapped. Another said, "It's all settled; we, the Punahou boys, will be the lunas and the McKinley fellows

The planters and the government of Hawaii welcomed women immigrants. Men with wives and families were thought to be steadier, more reliable workers than single men.

95

A Hawaiian family of Filipino descent in the 1920s. Hawaii offered rural people in the Philippines a way out of poverty and landlessness.

[students at a mostly Asian high school] will carry the cane." Young Asian Americans, however, did not want to be cane carriers. They set their sights on other goals, and this worried the planters.

Many planters did not think that laborers' children should be educated beyond the sixth or eighth grade. Planters urged the schools to offer vocational training, not literature courses. In other words, planters wanted Asian American children to get just enough education to prepare them for plantation jobs—but not enough to make them ambitious. A sugar company official argued that public school teachers should not keep their students from working on the plantations. If the schools continued to encourage the students to set high goals for themselves, the official warned, "we had better change our educational system here as soon as possible."

One planter complained about the cost of the public school system, saying, "Why blindly continue a ruinous system that keeps a boy and girl in school at the taxpayers' expense long after they have mastered more than sufficient learning for all ordinary purposes?" A visitor from the mainland, seeing Japanese children on the plantations, asked a

Maui planter whether he thought the new generation of Japanese would make intelligent citizens. "Oh, yes," the planter replied, "they'll make intelligent citizens all right enough, but not plantation laborers—and that's what we want."

In school, Asian Americans were getting an education that made them critical of the plantations. Teachers who had moved to Hawaii from the mainland taught the children of immigrant workers about American ideals: freedom, equality, and democracy. The youngsters recited the Gettysburg Address and the Declaration of Independence. They were taught that honest labor, fair play, and industriousness were virtues. But they "saw that it wasn't so on the plantation." There, equality did not exist. Haoles were on the top, and Asians were on the bottom. Comparing what they were learning in school with what they saw on the plantations, the students knew that something was wrong.

Seeing their parents suffer from drudgery, low wages, and prejudice, many second-generation Asians did not want to become plantation laborers themselves. They disliked the "plantation pyramid," which awarded the highest status to whites, and they also yearned to be something more than field laborers. My father, Toshio Takaki, who had come to the Puunene Plantation from Japan at the age of 13, felt the same restlessness as many Nisei, or second-generation Japanese. He worked as a field laborer at first, but he had an artistic passion and developed an interest in photography. An old friend recalled, "The cottages in camp were small and he used the closet as a darkroom." He went around the plantation carrying a camera and taking pictures. The plantation could not hold him down, and he left to study photography in Honolulu. He first worked for a photographic supply company in Honolulu, and later he opened his own photography studio.

A majority of the students at McKinley High School in Honolulu were the children of Asian immigrants. In 1922, boys at McKinley were asked what they hoped to be in the future. Most said they wanted to be skilled workers or professionals. A few hoped to become farmers. Only one-half of 1% said they planned to become laborers. "My father was a common laborer on a plantation, who worked every day from six in the morning to four o'clock in the afternoon," said a Japanese youth. "Whenever I saw some businessman in town, well dressed and gentle, my ambition was to become a businessman, and I was jealous of those who had high positions."

A Korean student explained that young Asians had been born with "yellow skins and educated as if their skins were white." To send a young man through high school and then ask him to labor in the fields, he added, was an "absurdity." Second-generation Asians knew they were American citizens. They resented being told that they were "not fit to be anything but plantation laborers." In 1928, the governor of Hawaii urged social workers to direct the Asian-American youth back to agriculture. A young Chinese man responded: "You cannot force the oriental youth with a high school education to go back to the plantations. He will not do it. We realize that our parents started on the plantations, but you cannot expect us to go back."

Education, many Asians believed, was the key to better jobs and freedom from the plantations. "Father made up his mind to send his children to school so far as he possibly could," said the daughter of a Japanese plantation worker.

"Yet he had no idea of forcing us. Instead he employed different methods which made us want to go to school. We were made to work in the cane fields at a very early age. . . . After a day's work in the fields dad used to ask: 'Are you tired? Would you want to work in the fields when you are old enough to leave school?' . . . My father did everything in his power to make us realize that going to school would be to our advantage."

Through education, the children and grandchildren of immigrants could enter a new world of words and ideas. A second-generation Japanese American mother wrote to her son who had gone away to college on the mainland: "It's 8:00 P.M. as I sit writing to you. About 1:00 A.M. in Ohio and I imagine you are snug in bed. We are still down at the store since Dad has to catch up soaking the teriyaki steak, etc. This week has been very busy and I am exhausted." She and her husband worked for 12 hours a day, seven days a week. To send their son away to college on the mainland caused a financial hardship. She herself had quit school after the eighth grade to work and help her parents. "I never went to school much and you can say that again," she wrote. "What I do know is from reading. . . . In my small way I am trying and doing my best (working) so that you being an exception *can and must* be above our intellectual level. At times I yearn for rest (6 years without a vacation)."

Her parents and other immigrants had labored as plantation workers to build the great sugar industry of Hawaii. They had made it possible for the American-born generations to have greater educational and employment opportunities. Years earlier, when they first saw the plantations and the dreary camps, they had been uncertain about their future in the islands. "Here you couldn't see anything, no view, no landscape, just fields and hills," one of them complained. "Ah, such a place. Is Hawaii a place like this?" Confused, many immigrants had asked in quiet moments of reflection:

> *Should I return to Japan?*
> *I'm lost in thoughts*
> *Here in Hawaii.*

And what would happen if they stayed too long?

> *Two contract periods*
> *Have gone by*
> *Those who do not return*
> *Will end up as fertilizer*
> *For the cane.*

In the evenings, sitting on their porches in the camps, the workers complained about the mean haole lunas, the way they were called by their bango numbers rather than their names, and the long, hard hours in the fields. But they refused to allow these things to rule their lives. Over the years, their feelings toward Hawaii had begun to change. As they worked in the fields, they saw how their labor had transformed and enriched the new land. "With my bare hands and calloused heart and patience," a Filipino worker boasted, "I helped build Hawaii."

When Asian workers went out on strike, they learned that they could improve the conditions of their communities and turn the camps into homes for their families. Japanese

workers, striking for higher wages, knew that their action was *kodomo no tami ni,* "for the sake of the children." And as Asian workers watched their children grow up and play in the camps, they began thinking of themselves as settlers and of Hawaii as their home. No longer did they dream of returning across the sea to Asia. They had created new futures for themselves and their children.

A Korean family in Hilo, Hawaii, in 1910. Many of the Korean immigrants had fled political turmoil and persecution in their homelands.

Japanese American volunteers, recruits for the 442nd Regimental Combat Team, prepare for service in World War II, which pitted the United States against Japan. Japanese Americans on the mainland were treated like political prisoners; most of those in Hawaii escaped this fate.

Chapter Nine

World War II in Hawaii

"ONE MORNING—I THINK IT WAS A SUNDAY—WHILE I was working at Palama Shoe Factory I heard, 'Pon! pon! Pon! pon!'" recalled a Japanese resident of Hawaii. He was only a few miles away from the U.S. navy base at Pearl Harbor. "I was drinking coffee and I thought, 'Strange. Are they having military practice?' At the corner of Liliha and Kuakini streets, a bomb fell in the back of a cement plant. We felt like going to see what happened, the noise was so loud. We found out that the war had started."

The bombs that fell on Hawaii on December 7, 1941, echoed loudly on the American mainland. Japan had bombed Pearl Harbor, killing more than 2,000 people and destroying many military ships and planes. Americans were stunned and angered by this attack on their territory. World War II was raging in Europe, but the United States had not yet entered the war. After the attack on Pearl Harbor, however, the United States promptly declared war on Japan—a war which was to last three and a half years.

In the wake of Pearl Harbor, many Americans felt hostility toward everything and everyone Japanese. On the mainland, more than 120,000 people of Japanese descent were interned—that is, rounded up and put into camps. Many of them had been born in the United States and were therefore American citizens. The Japanese people of Hawaii were spared this nightmare. While Asians on the mainland had remained "strangers" in a mostly white society, the Japanese and other Asians in the islands had become "locals." About 158,000 people of Japanese descent lived in Hawaii, making up 37% of the islands' population.

Shortly after inspecting the still-smoking ruins at Pearl Harbor, Navy Secretary Frank Knox declared that the Japanese in Hawaii had helped plan and carry out the attack. He was wrong. Investigators from the military intelligence organizations and the Federal Bureau of Investigation (FBI) all agreed that no sabotage had occurred. But Knox's alarming announcement fueled rumors of sabotage committed by Japanese Americans in the islands. Rumor said that Japanese plantation laborers had cut arrows in the sugar cane and pineapple fields to guide the Japanese bombers to the military installations, and that Japanese in Hawaii had given signals to enemy planes. Several weeks after the attack, Knox recommended that the Japanese of Oahu be rounded up and interned on one of the outer islands.

Knox's plan was blocked by General Delos Emmons, the military governor of Hawaii. Emmons declared in a radio broadcast, "There is no intention or desire on the part of the federal authorities to operate mass concentration camps. No person, be he citizen or alien, need worry, provided he is not connected with subversive elements. . . . While we have been subjected to a serious attack by a ruthless and treacherous enemy, we must remember that this is America and we must do things the American Way. We must distinguish between loyalty and disloyalty among our people."

Emmons also told the U.S. War Department that it would be a mistake to intern the Japanese of Oahu. The construction materials and workers that would be needed to build internment camps were more urgently needed for other wartime tasks, and soldiers could not be spared to guard the Japanese. He also pointed out that the Japanese were vitally important on Oahu. More than 90% of the carpenters, most of the transportation workers, and many of the plantation laborers were Japanese. If they were taken from their jobs, the island's economy would suffer. Japanese labor, Emmons said, was "absolutely essential" for rebuilding the military base at Pearl Harbor.

Emmons argued that the Japanese workers were indispensable and that the "Japanese question" should be handled "by those in direct contact with the situation." He believed he was in a better position to assess the threat from the local Japanese population than were the War Department officials, who were far away in Washington, D.C.

General Emmons remained at odds with the War Department, which continued to urge that "all the Japs" should be interned or relocated. In the end, Emmons had his way. He had seen no military reason for mass evacuation. Under his orders, only 1,444 Japanese were interned as potential threats to military security. Emmons was able to resist the federal government's pressure for mass internment partly because the people of Hawaii refused to treat the Japanese among them as enemies.

A few isolated local businessmen did favor mass relocation—not just for reasons of military security, but because they were afraid the Japanese were becoming too powerful in Hawaii. "At least 100,000 Japanese should be moved to inland mainland farming states," a telephone company official wrote to a navy admiral in August 1942. "If such a step as this was taken . . . not only the danger of internal

About 1,500 Japanese and Japanese American people were interned in this camp in Hawaii, but the U.S. War Department originally wanted to intern or evacuate ten times that many.

trouble could be avoided, but the future of Hawaii would be secured against the sure political and economic domination by the Japanese within the next decade."

But most of Hawaii's *kamaaina haoles* (whites who had been in the islands a long time) were against mass internment. The president of the Honolulu Chamber of Commerce called for fair treatment of the Japanese in Hawaii, saying, "There are 160,000 of these people who want to live here because they like the country and like the American way of life. . . . The citizens of Japanese blood would fight as loyally for America as any other citizen. I have read or heard nothing in statements given out by the military, local police or F.B.I. since December 7 to change my opinion. And I have gone out of my way to ask for the facts." The haole elite had a long history of interacting with the Japanese in the islands and were unwilling to permit their mass uprooting. Moreover, planters knew that the evacuation of more than one-third of Hawaii's population would destroy the sugar economy of the islands.

Like the business community, politicians and public officials urged restraint and reason. Hawaii's congressional delegate said that nothing should be done beyond arresting known spies. The Honolulu police captain denied rumors of Japanese snipers firing on American soldiers during the attack on Pearl Harbor. So did the head of the FBI in Hawaii, who said, "I want to emphasize that there was no such activity in Hawaii before, during or after the attack on Pearl Harbor. . . . I was in a position to know this fact. . . . Nowhere under the sun could there have been a more intelligent response to the needs of the hour than was given by the entire population of these islands."

When Hawaii's schools were reopened in January 1942, the school superintendent sent a message to all teachers:

> Let us be perfectly frank in recognizing the fact that the most helpless victims, emotionally and psychologically, of the present situation in Hawaii will be children of Japanese ancestry and their parents. The position of loyal American citizens of Japanese ancestry and of aliens who are unable to become naturalized, but who are nonetheless loyal to the land of their adoption, is certainly not enviable. Teachers must do everything to help the morale of these people. Let us keep constantly in mind that America is not making war on citizens of the United States or on law-abiding aliens within America.

The press in Hawaii also behaved responsibly. Newspaper editors expressed confidence in the loyalty of the local Japanese, and they criticized the internment of the Japanese on the mainland. "It was an invasion of the rights of the Japanese citizens on the Pacific coast to be picked up and shipped to

Japanese American staff members at a Honolulu hospital, working overtime after the bombing of Pearl Harbor. Hawaiians of Asian descent contributed greatly to the war effort.

In a farewell ceremony, a Japanese American soldier receives a lei, the flower necklace traditionally used in Hawaiian greetings and good-byes.

the interior," wrote one editor. Newspapers also cautioned their readers not to listen to rumors, or spread them. Within days after the attack on Pearl Harbor, a Honolulu paper dismissed rumors of Japanese sabotage in the islands as "weird, amazing, and damaging untruths." A magazine called *Paradise of the Pacific* warned readers, "Beware of rumors always, avoid them like a plague and, when possible, kill them as you would a reptile. Don't repeat for a fact anything you do not know is a fact."

There were many reasons why Hawaii refused to intern its Japanese. Dollars and cents provided a strong reason—the business community did not want its labor force disrupted. Furthermore, the people of Hawaii had developed a multicultural society that included Americans of Japanese ancestry.

The Japanese residents of Hawaii showed that they considered themselves to be Japanese *Americans*. During the morning of the attack, 2,000 second-generation Japanese who were serving in the U.S. Army in Hawaii fought to defend Pearl Harbor against enemy planes. Thousands of Japanese American civilians participated in the island's defense. They rushed to their posts as volunteer truck drivers for the Citizens' Defense Committee. They stood in long lines in front of the hospital, waiting to give their blood to the wounded. Many of these civilians were Issei, first-generation immigrants. Yet, as one of them said, "Most of us have lived longer in Hawaii than in Japan. We have an obligation to this country. We are *yoshi* [adopted sons] of America. We want to do our part for America."

That night, as the people of the islands tensely waited in the darkness for the invasion they feared, thousands of

Japanese American members of the Hawaii Territorial Guard—young people from the high schools and the University of Hawaii—guarded the power plants, reservoirs, and important waterfronts. For them, there was simply no doubt how they viewed the event: Japan had attacked their country. "As much as we would hate to see a war between the United States and Japan," one Nisei had said in 1937, "and as much as we would hate to see the day come when we would have to participate in such a conflict, it would be much easier, for us I think, if such an emergency should come, to face the enemy than to stand some of the suspicion and criticism, unjust in most cases, leveled against us." Rather than be suspected of disloyalty, he would "pack a gun and face the enemy." Four years later, that day did come—and thousands of Nisei stood tall in defense of their country.

"Japan's dastardly attack leaves us grim and resolute," declared Shunzo Sakamaki of the Oahu Citizens Committee for Home Defense four days after Pearl Harbor. "There is no turning back now, no compromise with the enemy. Japan has chosen to fight us and we'll fight." In December 1942, General Emmons asked for 1,500 Nisei volunteers for the army. More than 9,500 Nisei men answered Emmons's call. Many of them were sent to Camp Shelby, Mississippi, where they became members of the 442nd Regimental Combat Team. They gave their unit the slogan "Go For Broke," a phrase drawn from gambling on the plantations. "I wanted to show something, to contribute to America," explained Minoru Hinahara, who served as a Japanese language interpreter in the army's 27th Division. "My parents could not become citizens but they told me, 'You fight for your country.'" He, and many others, did exactly that.

Japanese and Filipino plantation workers united in a strike in 1946, shutting down most of Hawaii's plantations. The workers not only won higher wages and better conditions but also made a powerful demonstration of interethnic unity.

Chapter Ten

The Bloodless Revolution

THE WINDS OF WORLD WAR II BLEW A FRESH BREATH of democracy through America, opening the door for greater cultural diversity. After witnessing Nazi Germany's genocidal pogrom against the Jews, Americans became more aware of racism. Notions of white superiority were discredited. In the 1940s, several new laws and court decisions chipped away at racial discrimination and advanced civil rights for Asians and other minorities.

Reforms came not only from the president and the Supreme Court but also from the people themselves. In Hawaii, a bloodless revolution occurred in the labor movement. For a long time, plantation workers had been demanding their rights and a fair share of the wealth created by their labor. The war stirred unrest and agitation among them. Told that America had gone to war in defense of democracy, the laborers used their own democratic power to bring change to the workplace.

Before World War II, Asian plantation laborers had been largely left out of the democratic process. As aliens who could not become American citizens, Asian immigrants could not use the vote to advance their interests. Their only tool was the strike. But time had been on the side of the laborers. The Nisei, born in Hawaii, were citizens and were eligible to vote. In 1940, 31 out of every 100 Hawaiian voters were Japanese. They were the largest ethnic block among the voters.

By this time, the International Longshoremen's and Warehousemen's Union (ILWU) had begun organizing workers in Hawaii. ILWU planners soon recognized the laborers' potential political power. They decided to challenge the planter class at the ballot box first, then confront the bosses at the negotiating table. Their political strategy was to conduct voter registration drives on the plantations, elect their own representatives to the legislature, and seize political power from the sugar interests. The ILWU predicted that this strategy could easily swing Hawaii's legislature from "plantation management control to plantation worker control."

In a letter to the ILWU headquarters in San Francisco, regional director Jack Hall reported that less than 30% of union members who were eligible to vote were actually registered. "All emphasis at this time is on registration," he added. "We have a full time staff of four women in addition to some volunteer help for intensifying the registration drive. We can make a real dent in sugar control of our Legislature."

Months before the 1944 election, the ILWU leaders introduced political action committees, or PACs, to help

Jack Hall of the International Longshoremen's and Warehousemen's Union (ILWU). Hall helped organize Hawaiian plantation workers into ILWU chapters and encouraged them to use the power of their votes to bring about political change.

swing elections in favor of the workers. The PACs raised money for favored candidates and encouraged union members to vote for candidates who promised to support the goals of the union. In July 1944, Hall advised the PACs: "Every candidate for the Legislature . . . should be asked to make a written commitment to our program."

Meanwhile, at the local level, union leaders—Filipino, Japanese, Chinese, and Hawaiian—went "directly to their own groups," recalled an ILWU leader. "For example, Filipino guys would go out and talk to Filipino guys, house to house." After a union meeting, the workers would "break up into political rallies by language groups." At one of these rallies, workers were told, "Politics goes hand in hand with the labor movement. You got to strike together when it comes to voting." The message of the ILWU was clear: The voting booth would be the laborers' path to power.

On election day, most of the candidates supported by the ILWU PACs were elected to the House of Representatives and the Senate. The new lawmakers included ILWU members Joseph Kaholokula, Jr., of Maui and Amos Ignacio of the Big Island. "We really worked hard to get PACs candidates elected," said a Portuguese worker in 1945. The next spring the legislature passed a law that guaranteed plantation workers the right to collective bargaining. The way was now open for a major labor strike. Once the law was passed, the workers went out on strike for higher wages and a 40-hour work week.

The 1946 strike was different from earlier plantation strikes. As an ILWU newspaper explained, "This time, everybody is out with his union brothers and sisters—Japanese, Chinese, Filipino, Puerto Rican, Portuguese and Hawaiian.

Strikers' signs make their demands clear; decent housing, job security, better wages, and an end to racial discrimination.

We have a united front against our bosses and they are not able to pit one group of us against another as they did in the old days."

In all, 28,000 striking laborers shut down virtually all of Hawaii's plantations. After a long and bitter 79-day strike, the planters agreed to limit the work week to 40 hours. But the strike was important for more than just this victory. It was a landmark in interethnic unity. The ILWU announced, "It is the first time in the history of Hawaii that a strike of sugar workers has been conducted where there has been no split among racial groups."

Unity between ethnic groups, especially between Filipinos and Japanese, made sense. By the early 1940s, five out of ten laborers were Filipino, and three were Japanese. Labor leaders stressed the need for interethnic unity and cooperation. "The ILWU told the people," recalled one Filipino, "the ILWU is not looking at your ethnic background, racial background you had or what color you had. . . . The main fact is that we care only about you as a worker. As a worker, we have only one common goal."

The ILWU wanted all of the ethnic groups to be represented among the union's leadership in the islands. Local ILWU officers were told "to put Filipinos, Hawaiians, Portuguese and others into prominent positions, even though in some cases they might not be as qualified or as capable as the Japanese. It may well mean that Japanese of considerable ability may have to step back and press, instead, for the election of individuals of other racial groups."

An ILWU leader named Frank Thompson supervised the elections of local ILWU officers. Thompson's task was to force the integration of the union leadership, and he carried out his assignment with a heavy hand. If two Japanese were nominated in a row, Thompson would reject the second nomination, saying, "He's not eligible because my instructions are that we are going to have all nationalities. Pick somebody else but he can't be Japanese." Heavy-handed though it was, this "forced integration" worked. A list of the officers of local ILWU units reveals both Japanese and Filipino names.

The ILWU's strategy worked because the people of the islands were ready to cooperate across ethnic lines. For one thing, Japanese nationalism was no longer as strong as it had been. By the 1940s, 80% of the Japanese plantation laborers were Nisei. American citizens by birth, they did not have a close attachment to Japan. In school they sat next to Filipino, Chinese, Portuguese, and Korean children. They played games together, and they spoke in pidgin English. The new Nisei leaders were young, many of them in their twenties. "Most of our leadership in the various Locals and units," reported ILWU organizer Frank Thompson in 1944, "are young people and plenty intelligent. They don't intend to lead the same kind of existence that their Mothers and Fathers did when they were brought over here as coolie labor."

The Japanese and Filipinos of Hawaii did not need the mainland ILWU to teach them about the importance of interethnic solidarity. They had learned about standing together from their own experiences. "I came here in 1924," a Filipino worker told an interviewer in 1945. "I go out cut cane. Today, I still cut cane. I get $2 a day. Only enough for kau kau [food]. Nowadays, wartime, everything cost high—no can save. When they come ask me to join union, quick I join. I think union going help us. In 1924 Filipinos had strike for more pay, but that time only Filipinos strike. This time Filipino, Japanese, Portuguese, all join one union. More better that way."

A Japanese worker on the Olaa Plantation agreed. "We learned the idea of racial integration from experience," he explained. "We learned it from our experiences in the work place—in the fields and the mills—where day-to-day all races

Immigrants from Asia turned Hawaii's fertile fields into productive, profitable plantations. Through their shared labor, they created the plantation economy envisioned by their employers. But they also created something new and unexpected: a richly diverse, multicultural society.

worked on the job side-by-side. And so, when it came time to strike in 1946, the workers themselves knew they had to have what they called an 'all race strike.'" When they came together for the 1946 strike, the plantation workers of Hawaii achieved what some had envisioned back in 1920: a "big interracial union"—a true reflection of multicultural Hawaii.

"Lucky come Hawaii," some Asian immigrants whispered as they stood breathless with awe, watching rainbows arch over ancient volcanoes whose steep, forested sides hung from the clouds like green curtains. The islands gave these immigrants greater opportunities to make a place for themselves than their brethren found on the mainland. In Hawaii, they lived in a society where the elite class included Hawaiians, people with dark skin, and where racial divisions could not be drawn as sharply as on the continent. Because women immigrants were welcomed in Hawaii, Asians there were able to establish families sooner than their counterparts on the mainland. In their plantation camps, they had created communities that blended their old cultures in new ways.

Most important, unlike Asians on the mainland, the Asians in Hawaii were a majority of the population. On the continent, Asian immigrants found themselves competing with a large white working class, and they became victims of white working-class racism and violence. But on the islands, the Asians were able to weave themselves and their cultures into the very fabric of the islands, transforming their adopted land into a multicultural society, a place where they and their children would no longer be "strangers from a different shore."

Chronology

6th–13th centuries	Hawaii is settled by Polynesian seafarers.
1778	Captain James Cook of Britain is the first European to land in Hawaii, which he calls the Sandwich Islands.
1789	The first Chinese men arrive in Hawaii as sailors.
1795–1819	King Kamehameha rules a united Hawaiian kingdom.
1820	The first Christian missionaries arrive in Hawaii.
1835	William Hooper of Boston starts Hawaii's first sugar plantation.
1836	The first Chinese plantation laborers are employed in Hawaii.
1844	Hawaii is recognized as an independent nation by the United States, Great Britain, and France.
1850	Sugar planters form the Royal Hawaiian Agricultural Society to bring laborers from China.
1868	One hundred forty-nine Japanese laborers come to Hawaii.
1875	The Reciprocity Treaty allows Hawaii to sell sugar to the United States without paying

	import taxes, boosting the sugar industry in the islands.
1885	Large-scale immigration of Japanese workers begins.
1891	A strike by Chinese workers is brutally repressed by police.
1898	The United States takes possession of Hawaii and the Philippine Islands.
1900	Hawaii becomes a territory of the United States; the contract labor system is banned; the plantations are rocked by more than 20 labor strikes.
1906	Filipino emigration to Hawaii begins; Japanese workers strike successfully on the Waipahu Plantation.
1907	President Theodore Roosevelt prohibits Japanese workers from leaving Hawaii for the American mainland.
1909	On Oahu, 7,000 Japanese workers strike, demanding higher wages and equal pay for equal work.
1919	The Japanese and Filipino unions separately demand better wages and working conditions.
1920	Japanese and Filipino workers go on strike together; an interracial union called the Hawaii Laborers' Association is formed.
1940s	The International Longshoremen's and Warehousemen's Union (ILWU) recruits members from plantation workers of all nationalities.

1941	Japan bombs Pearl Harbor on December 7.
1944	Several ILWU members are elected to public office.
1946	An interethnic strike shuts down the plantations and wins a 40-hour work week for the laborers.
1959	Hawaii becomes a state.

Further Reading

Alcantara, Ruben. *Sakada: Filipino Adaptation in Hawaii.*
Washington: University of Washington Press, 1981.

Bird, Isabella. *Six Months in the Sandwich Islands.* 1890. Reprint.
Rutland, VT: Tuttle, 1990.

Burrows, Edwin G. *Hawaiian-Americans: An Account of the Mingling
of Japanese, Chinese, Polynesian, and American Cultures.* New
Haven, CT: Yale University Press, 1947.

Char, Tin-Yuke. *The Sandalwood Mountains: Readings and Stories of
the Early Chinese in Hawaii.* Honolulu: University of
Hawaii Press, 1975.

Glick, Clarence. *Sojourners and Settlers: Chinese Immigrants in
Hawaii.* Honolulu: University of Hawaii Press, 1980.

Gray, Francine du Plessix. *Hawaii: The Sugar-Coated Fortress.*
New York: Random House, 1972.

Inouye, Daniel. *Journey to Washington.* Englewood Cliffs, NJ:
Prentice-Hall, 1967.

Miyamoto, Kazuo. *Hawaii: End of the Rainbow.* Rutland, VT:
Tuttle, 1968.

Murayama, Milton. *All I Asking for Is My Body.* Honolulu:
University of Hawaii Press, 1989.

Okahata, James, ed. *A History of Japanese in Hawaii.* Honolulu:
United Japanese Society of Hawaii, 1971.

Perrin, Linda. *Coming to America: Immigrants from the Far East.*
New York: Delacorte, 1980.

Reimers, David M. *The Immigrant Experience*. New York: Chelsea House, 1989.

Saiki, Patsy Samie. *Sachie: A Daughter of Hawaii*. Honolulu: Kisaku, 1980.

Shirota, Jon. *Lucky Come Hawaii*. New York: Bantam, 1965.

Takaki, Ronald. *Pau Hana: Life and Labor in Hawaii*. Honolulu: University of Hawaii Press, 1983.

Wilson, Robert A., and Bill Hosokawa. *East to America: A History of the Japanese in the United States*. New York: Morrow, 1980.

Index

PICTURE CREDITS

RONALD TAKAKI, the son of immigrant plantation laborers from Japan, graduated from the College of Wooster, Ohio, and earned his Ph.D. in history from the University of California at Berkeley, where he has served both as the chairperson and the graduate advisor of the Ethnic Studies program. Professor Takaki has lectured widely on issues relating to ethnic studies and multiculturalism in the United States, Japan, and the former Soviet Union and has won several important awards for his teaching efforts. He is the author of six books, including the highly acclaimed *Strangers from a Different Shore: A History of Asian Americans,* and the recently published *A Different Mirror: A History of Multicultural America.*

REBECCA STEFOFF is a writer and editor who has published more than 50 nonfiction books for young adults. Many of her books deal with geography and exploration, including the three-volume set *Extraordinary Explorers,* recently published by Oxford University Press. Stefoff also takes an active interest in environmental issues. She served as editorial director for two Chelsea House series—*Peoples and Places of the World* and *Let's Discover Canada.* Stefoff studied English at the University of Pennsylvania, where she taught for three years. She lives in Portland, Oregon.